Secrets of a Jeweler

Shhh... your jeweler's listening!

Izzy Heller

authorHOUSE

AuthorHouse™
1663 Liberty Drive
Bloomington, IN 47403
www.authorhouse.com
Phone: 1-800-839-8640

This book is a work of non-fiction. Unless otherwise noted, the author and the publisher make no explicit guarantees as to the accuracy of the information contained in this book and in some cases, names of people and places have been altered to protect their privacy.

© 2005-2010 Izzy Heller. *All rights reserved.*

No part of this book may be reproduced, stored in a retrieval system, or transmitted by any means without the written permission of the author.

First published by AuthorHouse   06/28/2005-2010

ISBN: 978-1-4208-2612-8 (sc)
ISBN: 978-1-4208-2613-5 (hc)

Printed in the United States of America
Bloomington, Indiana

This book is printed on acid-free paper.

ABOUT THIS BOOK

In this recollection of work and play, Izzy Heller brings to life some of the interesting people he has met and the experiences he has had in the course of his professional lifetime as an upscale jeweler in the Washington, D.C. area.

Behind-the-scenes anecdotes in *Secrets of a Jeweler* open a window to some of the rich and famous and alas, also to some of the infamous in the capital city of the Western World.

THANKS

To my wife, partner and friend, Zelda, with whom I have traveled for 47 quick years, I am very indebted and grateful for the encouragement in this endeavor.

To my daughter, Tania, and my daughter-in-law, Loren for their valuable suggestions.

To my son, Leon, and my son-in-law, Sam, for their support.

To my manager, Nancy Spitzer, for keeping me and my manuscript on track. Also for her "Happy Thanksgiving" paintings which I am proud to own.

To Nancy P. Marriott for her sound advice as to publication.

To Demmy Williams, Fishel Beigel, Irene Pollin, the Didden Brothers, Dorothy K. Gordon, Mr. and Mrs. Judson C. French, Saul Goldberg, Ruth St. John, Nancy P. Marriott, all of whom allowed their names to be used in this work.

To John J. Kennedy of the Jewelers' Security Alliance for research on an incident.

To Blount Corp and Alan Bolesta for photographs.

To Kevin Tierney of Sotheby's for his kind assistance.

To the Worshipful Company of Goldsmiths for permission to use the image of the façade of Goldsmiths' Hall, London (publication "The Hallmark Silver Selection 1987").

DEDICATION

To the next generation of Story Tellers:

Daniel

Ariel

Gabi

Ben

Contents

DEDICATION vii
YOU SHOULD WRITE A BOOK! 1
IN THE BEGINNING 10
TRAIN, TRAIN AND TRAIN AGAIN 29
INCOGNITO 32
TWO WEDDING RINGS 37
JUSTICE BE DONE 45
THE WHITE HOUSE 49
HIS EXCELLENCY OUT OF AFRICA 51
OUR FRIEND, LENA 54
THE SHERATON SYSTEM 57
QE2 59
$3.25 MILLION 64
CUSTOMERS WHO STEAL 68
THE GRAVY TRAIN 72
THE BOUCHERON BRACELET 77
DAN, DAN THE LADIES MAN 81
MASTER SMITH ET AL 83
RED IS GREEN 85
FAIR COMPENSATION? 90
MY GENERAL MANAGER 92
THE TIFFANY NAME 99
THERE'S NO BUSINESS LIKE SHOW BUSINESS 104
DIVORCE, SOUTH AFRICAN STYLE 112
HIS OWN WORST ENEMY 114
THE TOKYO CONNECTION 116
RULE BRITTANIA 119

MAKING WAVES	129
LADIES, LADIES EVERYWHERE	136
THE DDC OF NYC	140
WHAT'S IT WORTH?	144
HARRY THE PLUNDERER	148
ARABIAN NIGHT	152
SAINT ROBERT, the gentile ZIONIST	154
THE BOYS FROM BEIRUT	159
THREE GLASS MEN	166
PAUL THE PATRIOT	169
NANCY PEERY	173
A LADY AND HER HAMMERS	178
THE KING OF BANKRUPTCY	183
MY BANKERS, GOD BLESS THEM!	185
MY DANCING PARTNER	192
ETHICS IN THE JEWELRY TRADE	198
MY RIGHT HAND	202
GO WELL!	209
About the Author	211

YOU SHOULD WRITE A BOOK!

"Plan your life, live your plan." Seems simple enough. But life is complex and offers many surprises. Thank goodness. Otherwise it would be so boring.

The unpredictability and the brevity of our existence make it all so exciting. There is an urgency, for me at least, to conquer, to do things while I'm still around.

I was born near Cape Town, so I am an African by birth. In 1980, at age 46, I immigrated to Washington, D.C. and became an American. That makes me . . . an African American.

Earlier, when I was 21 years old, I visited the States to obtain information for a thesis I was writing on the grain trade. If someone had told me then that a quarter of a century later, I would move here permanently and be in the jewelry business, I would have replied with a curt "IMPOSSIBLE."

My wife, Zelda, was born in Cape Town and like me, graduated from the University of Cape Town. When she was 19 and I was 23, we married and "planned our lives." Nothing in our plans included the U.S.A., which to us then was a million miles away.

I am the second of four sons: Jos, Izzy (that's me), Ralph and Charles. My Dad, Sam, my three brothers and I were all in the grain business. We made flour, split peas, pearl barley and animal feeds. We were successful and our corporation became public with a quotation on the Johannesburg Stock Exchange. Life was good. Life was forever.

But life is complex. "The winds of change are blowing in South Africa," said British Prime Minister, Harold McMillan on his official visit to Cape Town. As a family, all against the brutal system known as Apartheid, we decided to leave. We were only too aware what that meant. Giving up our privileged way of life, starting all over in a country with different laws, customs and culture. Leaving our loved ones behind.

We sold our businesses and homes for pennies on the dollar and put the proceeds into blocked South African rand accounts which the government controlled. With the passage of time, each rand depreciated from 135 US cents to 10 cents.

Today the four sons are in four separate businesses, but we have one thing in common. We are individualists. We do not work for anyone. We do our own thing.

Perhaps if we had really known the trauma of the emigrant, we would have stayed at home. "If you want home cooking," says the sign at the Carnegie Deli in New York, "stay home."

To change countries is not easy. South Africa said to us: "Go, but leave your assets here." America said: "If you are a Cuban asylum inmate, you can come on a refugee status. But if you wish to establish a business, give gainful employment to many and pay plenty in taxes, you'll have many hurdles to overcome and it will take many years to get a green card."

In the process of working with immigration attorneys in D.C., depression would set in. I would say to Zelda: "This is degrading. They've asked for the same information ten times now. Enough, tell them to shove their card." She would encourage me to be patient and we would cough up another few thousand dollars in legal fees.

To settle in a new land, psychiatrists will tell you, is traumatic. To settle without your family and friends, without your home, your furnishings, photographs etc. is to max out on the trauma scale. More so for a woman, who has an innate "nesting instinct." This instinct manifested itself in fainting spells for Zelda in her first year on American soil. Numerous medical tests confirmed her physical fitness and yet she would faint in a mall, in a restaurant, wherever. Only when we established a home and our children arrived to join us, did Zelda's fainting become a thing of the past.

In those early days in a new country, two couples were most helpful. Our sponsors, Alma and Joe Gildenhorn (Ambassador Joseph B.), and our cousins, David and Yona (Heller) Goldberg, were our lifelines in America. They entertained us, they introduced us to people (including our C.P.A., Jerry Gross) and generally "showed us the way." We try to reciprocate their kindness in our support for new immigrants.

On their respective arrivals in Washington, our two children enrolled at Georgetown University – Tania, as a M.D. who had re-written her finals in the U.S. and now had to do her residency, and Leon, who was an undergraduate overseas and now transferred to obtain a degree in business and a C.P.A. qualification.

Both kids did well and have made a mark for themselves in their respective careers. They have married and each couple has two children. Our four grandchildren (all born in the U.S.A.) can qualify as candidates for the presidency of the U.S.

As I have said, my background was in grain. Zelda was a schoolteacher who had entered into the wonderful world of the international antique business.

Although I was offered executive positions by my friends in the U.S. grain trade, I decided I would throw my lot in a small pond where hopefully I would become a big fish.

On October 28, 1980, Zelda and I opened "Heller Antiques Ltd." (trading as Heller Jewelers) in the Barlow Building at 5454 Wisconsin Avenue, Chevy Chase, Maryland. We were so close to the boundary of the District of Columbia I could, in those days, when I was younger and stronger, have driven a golf ball from my front door in one state to beyond Western Avenue in another.

So in my middle age, I went back to school and studied silver, jewelry, diamonds and appraising at the Gemological Institute of America, Indiana University, the American Silver Guild and the International Society of Appraisers. I attended trade shows. I read books and more books. When I was invited to speak, I felt like the blind leading the blind. I must have appeared authoritative, because I became a lecturer in demand.

Our business which started on a shoe-string, grew by leaps and bounds. Perhaps it was that we spoke differently. Time and again our clients would comment our accents were so civilized, so British! We expanded the store twice and our exquisite inventory – acquired privately, from estates, trade shows and dealers in the States, Europe and Asia – was much appreciated by our ever bigger and broader customer base. The multi-million dollar stock-in-trade we built up was always turning over. Buying to high standards was much more difficult than selling, we discovered.

Zelda and I made new friends. We were invited to dinner parties and were asked questions about our past in South Africa. "You should write a book" was the frequent response. We did. *Deadly Truth*. And later, when I volunteered some of our experiences about Heller Jewelers at the dinner table of our friends, "You should write a book" was the refrain. I did. You are holding it.

We are told robbers target banks because "that's where the money is." They also aim at jewelers because that's where the valuables are. Most people think diamond dealers are very rich. "They can afford it" is a slogan of many. Perhaps thieves rationalize this belief into justifying their illegal activity.

Security is a major concern to a jeweler. There are so many crooks around. Violence has followed theft and burglary. The insurance industry has suffered such losses in our industry that they specify rigid requirements to be adhered to before a claim can be validated. So we had to install high quality vaults with key, combination and time-control access, closed circuit television systems with video tape replays, buzzers and panic buttons, secret codes, open and closing precautions. We insisted on locked showcases and tight procedures. We bought kidnapping insurance.

We sustained regular losses. Even our customers and staff would steal from us. The losses because of "shrinkage" were a constant source of worry. Many of my stories here have to do with rampant dishonesty.

The Reid Psychological Company established a simple questionnaire system which would statistically identify applicants who were at high risk for theft. They claimed 90 percent accuracy. We certainly found this simple test was a great help in reducing "shrinkage" by staff. It was legal to ask that these questions be answered, provided all applicants were invited to do so. There could be no discrimination.

Through our business we have made friends all over the world. We can find them in the London Silver Vaults, the Manhattan Antique Center, Sotheby's Auction Gallery in New York, the Basel Jewelry Fair in Switzerland, the Via Condotti in Rome, the Champs Elysees in Paris and the Smithsonian Institution in Washington, D.C.

The joy of having an upscale business in the capital of the western world lies in meeting and befriending hundreds of delightful people.

One Saturday, we had Art Buchwald, Chris Wallace, Lesley Stahl, Pat Buchanan, and Judith Martin (Miss Manners) in our store. Other contacts were with diplomats, government leaders and scientists. After all, here was where 140 international embassies, the Smithsonian, the World Bank, the National Institutes of Health and dozens of well known institutions and associations are headquartered.

We were always mindful of the enrichment to our lives by being associated with the crème de la crème of our society. The opportunity to interact with knowledgeable and interesting people was a bonus we always appreciated.

And now after twenty-four years as a jeweler, I have taken a decision to phase down my business. My wife has a brilliant career as a realtor. Our daughter, the pediatrician, heads a clinic for eating disorders and is a successful author (three books published to date). Our son, the entrepreneur, is on to his third successful career, always on his own. First as an options trader, then as an internet service provider to students (remember Fastweb.com, now part of Monster.com) and presently in real estate. We gave our kids roots, now they have wings. I have no regrets they have not gone into the jewelry trade.

These words are an attempt to tell you about some of the more interesting events that occurred amidst the grueling 50 to 60 hour work-weeks over my first two decades in America. The life for this jewelry retailer was certainly not an easy one over that period (1980 – 2000). Nor for my wife, Zelda, who fortunately was by my side.

So in semi-retirement, and in old age, I have decided very modestly to chronicle some anecdotes of my experiences in my store, what one might call revealing "Secrets of a Jeweler." Except for some of the names and places, everything is true.

I hope you will find my stories interesting.

Izzy Heller

Washington, D.C.

heller.antiques1@verizon.net

Izzy Heller

IZZY AND ZELDA WITH THEIR HELLER LOGO

OUR CHILDREN AND GRANDCHILDREN
BACK ROW L TO R: ARIEL AND BEN.
CENTER ROW L TO R: DANIEL, TANIA AND SAM.
FRONT ROW L TO R: IZZY, ZELDA, GABI, LOREN AND LEON.

Secrets of a Jeweler

THE COVER OF OUR NOVEL *DEADLY TRUTH*. Painting by Judy Horowitz)

Izzy Heller

IZZY AND LEON TROUT FISHING IN MICHIGAN TO CELEBRATE A 70th

Secrets of a Jeweler

ALMA AND JOE GILDENHORN

DAVID AND YONA GOLDBERG

IN THE BEGINNING

The town of my birth, Worcester, South Africa, has a population of some 30,000 people and is situated about 70 miles north of Cape Town. The Breede River flows alongside the town, coming down from a volcanic ring of tall mountains.

Worcester comprises a beautiful series of valleys, many filled with magnificent vines. Deciduous fruit like peaches, apricots, pears and plums grow in abundance but the mainstay of the economy is grapes. There are canneries and grain processing facilities, built by my family, and chicken farms, which I introduced to the town.

This was a great place to live. Plenty of sunshine, a mild climate, clean air, pure water, friendly people of all color and a place where windows were left open and front doors unlocked.

Despite all this, it was an adjustment in 1958 for the newlywed Zelda to come from the big city of Cape Town (predominately English speaking) to the sleepy village of Worcester, which was overwhelmingly Afrikaans. I had an option to buy a small farm about 10 miles out of town, a paradise of a place that had some animals, orchards, a vineyard and a modest house. I sensed it was too much to ask from her and I let the option lapse. We started life in a town flat, part of a low rise apartment complex known as Quentin Court, which I was later to own.

My wife's father and her uncle were into manufacturing and retailing new furniture. Yet her preference in decorating the 1,200 square feet which we called home ran to antiques. This endeavor presaged a lifelong love for beautification of home interiors.

Zelda has always had boundless energy. With her university majors in Psychology and Science she secured a teaching position at the School for the Blind, where an illogical policy mandated married women could not enjoy tenure. Twelve months later, when a single woman applied for the post, Zelda was terminated in favor of the preferential applicant. Unemployed, she could devote more time to the joy of the world of antiques.

She scoured the town and the surrounding districts for old Cape Dutch furniture, hand-crafted from indigenous fruit woods and the prized and scarce yellow wood and stink wood.

Often she and her driver would return from a day in the countryside, her pickup truck laden with old treasures which were offloaded and squeezed into our tiny flat. Her modus operandi was to exchange new furniture for old and pay for any difference in value.

Friends would hear of my claustrophobia amidst the three-high stockpile of chairs and offer to reduce the density. Zelda would oblige and sell the surplus items. She had commenced trading.

When the inventory became unbearably large, I bought her an old Georgian house on a corner of High Street for an antique business, and so Zelda's RUSBANK GALLERY was born.

Soon she became known to pay top prices for antiques and the result was sellers brought her truckloads of "the stuff." She could afford to be picky about quality. Her store became a treasure house and a destination for collectors from all over South Africa. Her advertising slogan was "Rusbank Gallery, the store that's making Worcester famous" and it was true.

In addition to furniture, Rusbank Gallery stocked a comprehensive range of antiques. In particular, were magnificent displays of English jewelry and Cape (early South African) silver. Most of the Cape silver was in the hands of institutions. Very little was owned by private collectors. Some years later, Zelda decided to "go" for whatever was offered, whether brought to her or offered at public auction.

The leading newspaper *The Star* reported as follows on January 25, 1974:

"I have reason to believe that Zelda Heller of Worcester has just made one of the biggest 'killings' of recent years in Cape silver, that precious and rapidly dwindling item for the art lover and investor.

If it is not Zelda Heller who bought practically every top item of the 17 or so lots that came up at Ashbey's splendid auction of antique and modern silver and plate at their gallery in Church Street here last week, then I congratulate "Madam," as the auctioneer designated the buyer of the lots.

But in the meantime my compliments will be directed to Zelda. I firmly believe she was the lucky person who was able to spend most of the best part of R7 000 that was paid for the Cape silver at the auction."

Alas, when we left South Africa for the States, we were compelled to sell Zelda's important collection of Cape Silver. The only comfort was it went to good homes and museums in Johannesburg and Pretoria.

Our 1928 American Graham Paige roadster, for which our family won a coveted "Concours d' Elegante" award, suffered the same fate. We had a lot of fun with this car. It drew stares wherever we went. It required considerable force to turn the steering wheel and at 25 miles per hour one got "shook up." How it came to be in South Africa, we will never know. There was no other Graham Paige in the country to our knowledge.

The business grew and Rusbank Gallery opened a branch on Church Street in Cape Town. It became apparent importation would have to take place to adequately to feed the two stores, so Zelda undertook trips to England twice a year to buy English Georgian and Victorian jewelry and silver. I took time off from the grain business and accompanied her to act as adviser, security officer and driver.

Spending money is the fun part of any business. We enjoyed these overseas jaunts. We became known at Portobello Road, Bermondsey and the other London antique markets and established wonderful contacts. Our purchases were quickly freighted back home where eager buyers were waiting.

In terms of space requirements, jewelry and silver win hands-down against the bulkiness of furniture. More and more, Rusbank Gallery specialized in "valuable smalls."

In the late 1970's, when thoughts of leaving South Africa crossed our minds, our whole approach to things changed. Our "expansion" mode changed to a "phase down" policy and we began a process of slow but sure liquidation. It was very sad to put a brake on success. We had worked so hard to build up our client base.

We were not sure to which country we would emigrate. So we sent a container of South African antiques to Houston, Texas for sale as a test

Secrets of a Jeweler

to see whether we could hold our own in a foreign market. Zelda and I followed a month later.

The ship carrying our container was delayed 3 weeks, so with little to do but wait out its arrival, we got to know Houston and some Texans. Both got very high marks from us.

Finally the goods arrived and were marketed through the premises of a friendly antique dealer. We got a favorable write-up in the Houston Chronicle and we had a sell-out in ten days.

We were so encouraged by the friendly Americans and the success with the antiques we decided there and then: "America, here we come!"

Zelda and I returned to South Africa to wind up things and wait for green cards which finally arrived some two years after the Houston exhibition.

I did not fancy working as a junior executive in the grain business after running my own show. So I decided to join Zelda in an antique business in the city of Washington. Her knowledge of furniture, porcelain, glassware, jewelry and silver was the foundation on which our American dream was to be built.

In 1980, we threw ourselves into the challenge of our new venture with gusto. We were fortunate in getting considerable publicity free of charge from the *Washington Post* in a "Starting Over" article about our business and which featured the South African antiques in our home. Also helpful was a T.V. channel 5 segment on Chevy Chase shopping which showed off our store's beautiful jewelry to great advantage.

Nine months after we opened the store, we were lucky to acquire several Picasso platters. These silver dishes, about 17" in diameter had been designed by Pablo Picasso, who commissioned Francois Victor-Hugo, one of the top French silversmiths, to hand-craft a series for himself.

It is said Picasso initially kept the existence of these platters a secret and concealed them as though they were his private treasure. Subsequently he authorized Francois Hugo to make a small numbered edition of each for sale.

These striking objects d'art were illustrated in the *Washington Post* on Sunday, June 21, 1981 with a mention they were on exhibit at Heller Antiques.

The response was big and quick and the platters were soon sold at about $15,000 each.

After the first decade we had built up Heller Jewelers to the point where our double "L" logo was widely recognized and our company was a well-known and respected entity in the Nation's capital.

Then Zelda went solo, leaving me with Heller Jewelers while she embarked on a real estate career with the brokers, Long & Foster. Today she is number one in that company in the category "realtor with one assistant."

Secrets of a Jeweler

THE HELLER BROTHERS L TO R: JOS, CHARLES, IZZY AND RALPH.

Eighteen-year-old Solomon Heller, born of a family which had been associated with the milling industry for more than a century, arrived in Cape Town from Lithuania in 1920. He had one ambition: to establish his own mill in South Africa. In pursuit of this ideal, he took a job as a mill labourer with Daniel Mills and Sons in Cape Town and began a decade's struggle to accumulate sufficient funds for his own enterprise.

In 1932 Solomon Heller finally achieved his ideal with the opening of the Worcester Milling Company. His triumph was short lived; no sooner had the flour milling machinery been commissioned than the enterprise was caught up in the problems of the Great Depression. In 1934 the business was liquidated.

Solomon Heller continued his association with the grain trade as a broker and agent, and in 1940 again entered the milling industry through an interest in Joubert Mills of Lower Church Street, Worcester, in association with, among others, Mr T. C. Botha, of the farm *Stettyn*.

Mr Solomon Heller, founder of Victory Mills.

The first home of Victory Mills in Durban Street, Worcester.

MY DAD SOLOMON HELLER AND HIS ORIGINAL FLOUR MILL

A short while later Mr Heller took over Joubert Mills completely and also bought the business of Mr A. P. Botha in Durban Street, Worcester. With the assistance of Mr C. W. Everson of Slanghoek, Rawsonville, he merged the two concerns as Victory Mills – so named because the company's incorporation in 1945 followed the end of World War II and the Allies' triumph.

Initially Victory Mills milled wheat only, and produced coarser grades of flour. Over the years the product range was extended to include items like pearl barley and split peas, and eventually in an effort to utilise the wheaten offal, manufacture of animal feeds was started.

The business grew, Mr Heller was joined by his four sons, three of whom are still active in the business, and adjoining properties were acquired in Durban Street. With the growth came further changes. In 1958 Victory Mills sold its wheat mill to SASKO and began distribution of SASKO's flour and meal, an association which continues to this day.

The sale led to a new emphasis in the company's activities – an emphasis on the production and marketing of grain foods and feeds. The foods range was expanded, and with the opening on a large scale of supermarkets, Victory Mills pioneered pre-packing of the various grocery lines which hitherto had been weighed for the consumer by the retailer.

A further innovation helped reduce the cost of coffee-type beverages. Through the addition of pearl barley in the roasting process, fewer imported coffee beans were needed by manufacturers. These and other developments, based on the foundations laid by Mr Heller and his belief in "growth through service" helped establish Victory Mills not only as a major supplier of food and animal feeds but also as a substantial consumer of agricultural produce.

The '70s have brought further important developments. The company has achieved a major advance in cattle nutrition in the Republic by pioneering the process of micronisation, whereby cereals are cooked on a continuous basis by heat and infra red radiation. The process, discovered in the United States and developed in Great Britain, has made cooked cereal an economic reality for use in feeds and has yielded outstanding results.

In 1973 the Heller family exchanged its interests in Victory Mills for shares in Bechmalt Holdings Ltd, a company then listed on the Johannesburg Stock Exchange and which in turn was acquired by Federale Volksbeleggings in 1975. These transactions have opened new technical and marketing horizons for Victory Mills.

The days of automated feed mills were far removed in 1943 when Mr Carel Titus first joined Mr Solomon Heller in the milling business. Over three decades he has tended an increasingly sophisticated range of equipment and has seen, as the longest-serving employee, Victory Mills become a major supplier of food and animal feed.

"Featherlite Flour", a product of the Worcester Milling Company, which was Mr Solomon Heller's first enterprise.

MORE ABOUT THE HELLER MILLING BUSINESS

Secrets of a Jeweler

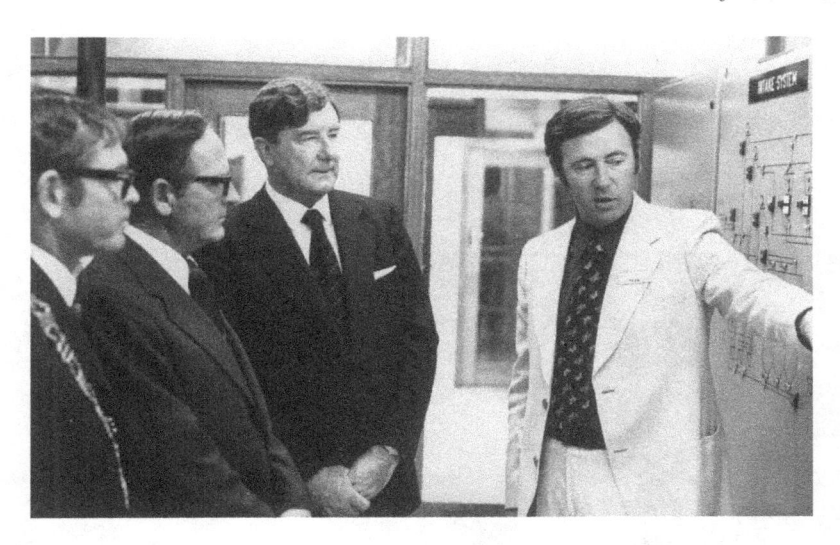

IZZY AT THE CONTROL PANEL WITH THE MINISTER OF FINANCE, THE MEMBER OF PARLIAMENT, AND THE MAYOR.

IZZY AT THE OPENING OF AN AUTOMATED FEED MILL WITH THE MINISTER OF FINANCE.

Izzy Heller

GRAIN SILOS AT THE WORCESTER MILL

Secrets of a Jeweler

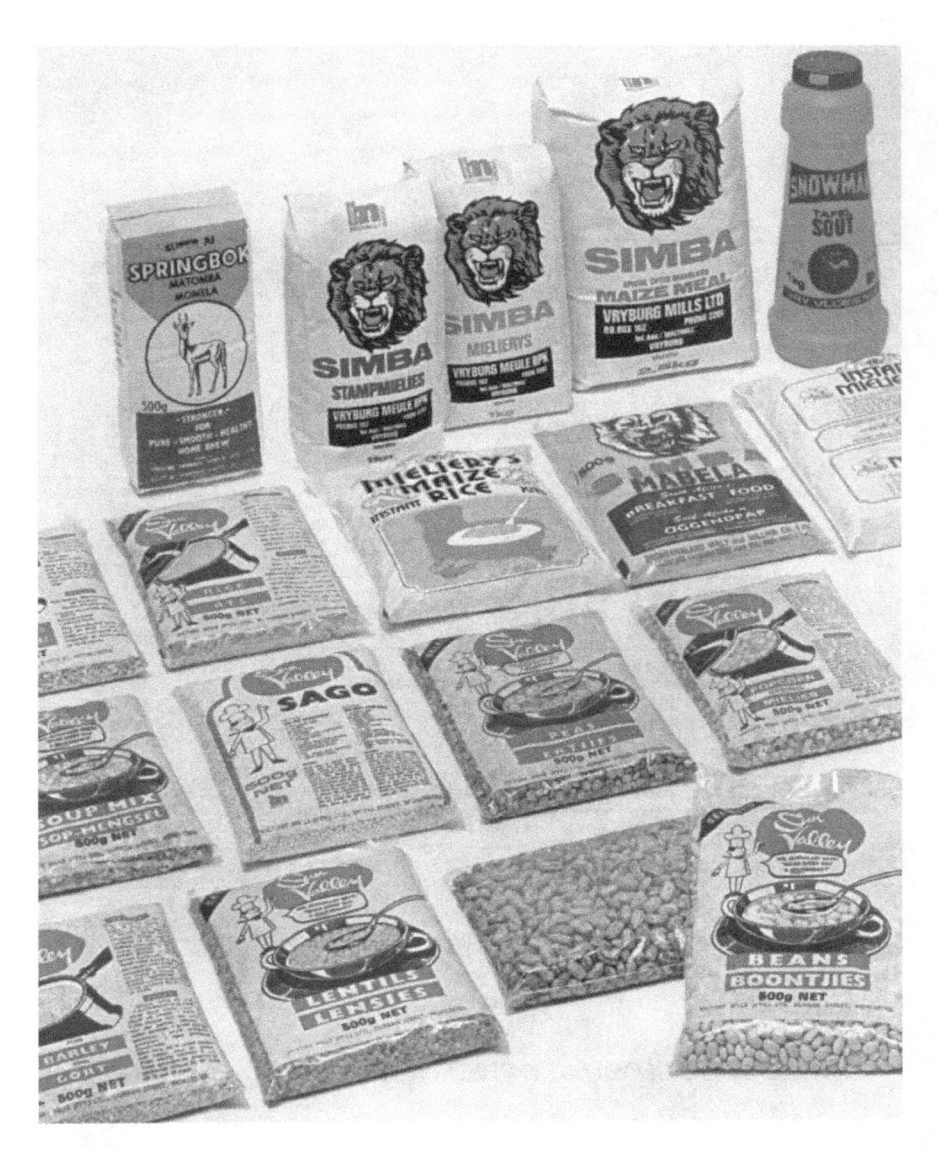

A VARIETY OF OUR FOOD AND FEED PRODUCTS

Izzy Heller

A VARIETY OF OUR FOOD AND FEED PRODUCTS

Secrets of a Jeweler

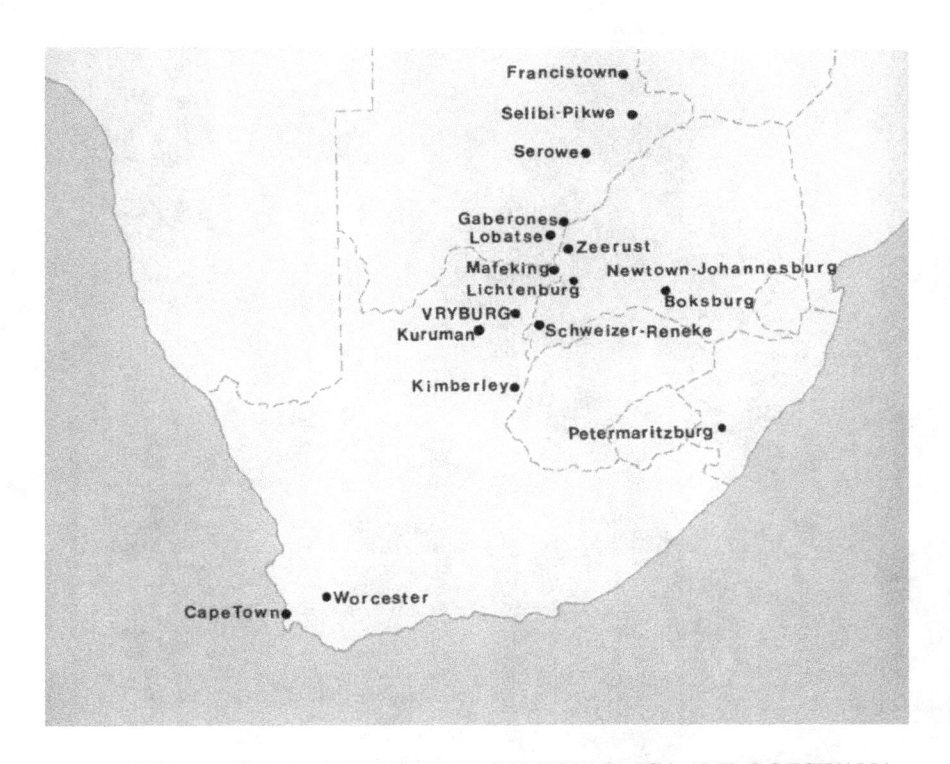

MAP SHOWING OUR FACTORIES IN SOUTH AFRICA AND BOTSWANA

Izzy Heller

Starting Over

Uprooted from their first home, Israel and Zelda Heller packed up their life to begin again

BY ANDY LEON HARNEY

Below, a Dutch "Kas" or cupboard with inlaid work, here in a classic combination of dark and yellow woods. When found by Heller, it had been painted over in an ugly green.

*I*f you decided it was time to pack up all your possessions and trek halfway across the world to another country, which of your goods would you take and which would you leave behind? Would you take practical objects—the mixing bowl, the bedding, the floor lamp? Or would you opt for the frivolous but memory-filled? An old baseball glove or a simple night table.

When Zelda and Israel Heller decided to move from their native South Africa and open an antique silver and jewelry shop in Washington, their government allowed them to depart with only a limited amount of their life's savings. They could, however, take most of their personal possessions accumulated in 22 years of marriage. For them, that was quite a lot. In the end, they left behind many

WASHINGTON POST ARTICLE ON OUR HOME

Secrets of a Jeweler

THE STAR JOHANNESBURG FRIDAY JANUARY 25 1974

Silver scoop at Ashbey's

ART AND INVESTMENT
Denis Godfrey

CAPE TOWN — I have reason to believe that Zelda Heller of Worcester has just made one of the biggest "killings" of recent years in Cape silver, that precious and rapidly dwindling item for the art lover and investor.

If it is not Zelda Heller who bought practically every top item of the 17 or so lots that came up at Ashbey's splendid auction of antique and modern silver and plate at their gallery in Church Street here last week, then I congratulate "Madam", as the auctioneer designated the buyer of the lots.

But in the meantime my compliments will be directed to Zelda. I firmly believe she was the lucky person who was able to spend most of the best part of R7 000 that was paid for the Cape silver at the auction.

However, I know for certain that a Johannesburg collector got one item — a Cape silver four-pronged konfyt fork by Lawrence Twentyman, circa 1820, for R80.

But Zelda Heller has definitely been around in the past week buying Cape silver. I first got on her trail when, visiting a shop where I was told I might find the only two pieces of Cape silver in a dealer's hands, I arrived too late. She had been the day before and bought both pieces.

Then began the slaughter by "Madam" at Ashbey's. Practically every major item auctioned was knocked down to the lady thus referred to, sitting two rows behind my wife and I at the sale. It was not Zelda Heller in person, but. . . .

* * *

Anyway, top price for the Cape silver was R950 for a Cape silver up the scalloped body with gilt interior and raised upon a shaped foot and having a shaped handle. It was a John Townsend item, circa 1824, and had the simulated English marks.

Next best price was R840 for a Cape silver covered bonboniere, the fluted lid with cast rose finial, and the body with shallow spiral flutes and small feet — by Jan Byleveld.

Another John Townsend item, another silver cup, made R700. It was smaller than his previous piece.

Three fiddle and thread tablespoons by Lawrence Twentyman, with simulated English marks, fetched R50 each, while six dessertspoons matching the tablespoons, were sold for R40 each. Six plain fiddle pattern table forks by William Moore, with simulated English marks, made R85 each, and six dessert forks by the same maker sold for R70 each. The final William Moore lot, four teaspoons, were sold for R40 each.

Two John Townsend teaspoons made R36 each, and a soup ladle by Frederick Waldeck sold for R280. A Johannes Combrinck sauce ladle made R190, and a soup ladle by the same maker was bid up to R400.

A set of 12 dessertspoons by Lawrence Twentyman sold for R50 each, making R600 for the lot, and a Johannes Combrinck soup ladle, fiddle pattern with shoulder, and the maker's mark with side rosettes, was knocked down for R400.

Eleven Cape silver table forks, fiddle pattern, by Willem Godfried Lotter sold for R45 each (R495), and a Lawrence Twentyman sauce ladle with simulated English marks went for R22. Finally, a snuff box, unmarked, but with the typical pricked designs, made R200.

* * *

Of the other silver at the sale, top price was R1 400 for a Paul Storr pair of silver sauce tureens. These Georgian pieces were boat-shaped on oval feet with gadroon rims, ring handles and engraved crests. They weighed 22oz each.

* * *

Second best price was R1 200 for a magnificent oval-shaped Georgian silver fruit basket, with crested centre, deep sides, flared rim and pierced in a scroll and leaf design with shaped hoop handles. Made in London in 1753 by S Herbert and Co, the weight was 46½ oz.

PRESS CLIPPING SHOWING OUR ATTEMPT TO CORNER THE SILVER MARKET

Izzy Heller

ZELDA AND LEON WITH HER GRAHAM PAIGE CAR

ZELDA WITH A CARRIAGE WHICH SHE SOLD FOR THE FOYER OF A JOHANNESBURG HOTEL

Secrets of a Jeweler

EARLY DAYS AT HELLER JEWELERS

INTERIOR OF THE STORE

HELLER ANTIQUES LTD.
Proudly Presents The
Picasso
SILVER PLATTERS

In 1967, Picasso commissioned Francois Victor Hugo, one of the most accomplished silversmiths in France, to execute a series of silver platters after his original models and designs. A small, numbered edition of each was duly made.

It is unnecessary to extol the merits of these memorable objets d'art. The genius of design, the manual dexterity, superb craftsmanship and artistic sensibility are fully in evidence.

Heller Antiques Ltd. is proud to announce that we now have for sale in our gallery a major portion of this series.

We cordially invite your inspection of the Picasso silver platters.

HELLER

HELLER ANTIQUES LTD.
5454 WISCONSIN AVENUE, CHEVY CHASE, MARYLAND 20015
(301) 654-0218

WASHINGTON POST ANNOUNCEMENT

Secrets of a Jeweler

PICASSO SILVER PLATTER

Izzy Heller

PICASSO SILVER PLATTER

TRAIN, TRAIN AND TRAIN AGAIN

These days, it is not uncommon to find a store's cashier talking on a cell phone or chewing gum while serving a customer. This is anathema to me.

I regarded every member of my staff as an ambassador of my business. This required inter alia, modest dress (no plunging necklines for women, no short sleeves for men), a cheerful disposition and product knowledge. Class and style were important to project the image of trust and confidence we required.

With each new recruit, I spent several hours on a one-on-one basis in my tiny office. I would go over the procedure manual and the specific job description. I handed out booklets. Whether a sales associate, a gemologist or telephonist, each was subjected to this meeting.

The response to the orientation was varied. One newcomer would study the material, blend in, carefully watch the old hands and swim on his or her own. Another would be totally apathetic and need a high voltage jolt of electricity to perform. And a third would over-confidently tell my customers an Eastern European cup was made by Faberge, even if it was not. (Misrepresentation was a crime in my book and I had to remind this party that saying "I do not know" is acceptable.) Only a few understood study or continuing education was essential to success and full enjoyment in the work place.

To follow up on the many lectures I gave at staff meetings, I would have questionnaires from time to time so progress could be monitored. Training became more interesting and challenging with these "tests."

Let's see how well you do on my basic SILVER QUIZ.

SILVER QUIZ - WHAT IS . . . . . ?

SILVER QUIZ - WHAT IS . . . . . ?

1. SILVER
2. STERLING
3. COIN SILVER
4. CONTINENTAL SILVER
5. 84 SILVER
6. QUADRUPLE SILVER
7. E.P.N.S.
8. OLD SHEFFIELD PLATE
9. CIRCA
10. LION PASSANT
11. LONDON HALLMARK
12. BIRMINGHAM HALLMARK
13. SHEFFIELD HALLMARK
14. SILVER PLATE
15. ANTIQUE
16. REPOUSSE
17. ENGRAVING
18. INSCRIPTION
19. CARTOUCHE
20. ARMORIAL
21. BEADING
22. CHASING
23. VICTORIAN
24. EDWARDIAN
25. GEORGIAN
26. DATE LETTERS
27. MONARCH'S HEAD
28. FLATWARE
29. HOLLOWARE
30. PATINA
31. VERMEIL
32. BRITANNIA STANDARD
33. ASSAY
34. GADROONING
35. JUDAICA
36. MENORAH
37. CHANUKAH LAMP
38. SPICE BOX
39. SALVER
40. PIERCING
41. ARGYLE
42. WINE COOLER
43. WINE COASTER
44. BERRY SPOON
45. MARROW SCOOP
46. GRAPE SHEARS
47. SIFTER SPOON
48. LADLE
49. ENAMEL
50. TONGS

Secrets of a Jeweler

Since you probably did well on the silver questions, allow me to pose these few on gems and jewelry.

<u>TEN LITTLE QUESTIONS.</u> (Here we give you a little help.)

1. A sapphire occurs in almost all colors except: <u>R . .</u>

2. An emerald is most closely related to another beryl: <u>A . . . .</u>

3. The rarest, hardest, most valuable gem in the world is a: <u>D . . . . . .</u>

4. Art Deco jewelry is from which century: <u>T . . . .</u>

5. A natural green color diamond gets its color from: <u>R . . . .</u>

6. The number of carats (diamond weight) in a gram is: <u>F . . .</u>

7. Which is more expensive per gram: Gold, Silver or Platinum? <u>P . . . . .</u>

8. How many facets does a round brilliant cut diamond have? <u>5 .</u>

9. The birthstone for the month of September is: <u>S . . . . . .</u>

10. Rank in order of diamond value: Synthetic, Natural, Simulant: <u>N . . . . . .</u>, <u>S . . . .</u>, <u>S . . . .</u>

With the clues, that quiz was surely much easier.

The penalty for ignorance or error in the jewelry business is generally much greater than in other retail establishments. The values are higher, credibility is more important and theft is a constant risk.

Occasionally we would have outside experts speak to our staff. We encouraged colleagues to enroll for courses with the Gemological Institute of America (G.I.A.) or to attend seminars, often on a subsidized basis.

As far as selling was concerned, even with training, passion was an essential trait. Without it, results were poor. Comparison between a bright gemologist who had the knowledge but lacked the magic "P" and a zealous salesperson of average intelligence proved the point. Enthusiasm made sales, period.

I enjoyed hypnotizing my staff at training sessions. I should have been a teacher.

INCOGNITO

With our name Heller on the door, just about everyone who graced our little place with their presence knew who we were.

Unfortunately the reverse did not hold true. Often we would see a familiar face, but not recollect the name. This became very embarrassing at times and on some occasions a VIP would visit and not be recognized.

The first such person was George Will, the famous syndicated columnist and brilliant TV debater. He found a Christmas gift soon after our store opened but could not find his credit card to pay. He was so charming and apologetic I said he could send us a check in due course. Mr. Will became a loyal if intimidating customer. Most of my staff were a little awestruck and scared to serve him. I got to know him over the years and learned of his knowledge and love of baseball. Often I would ask his opinion on some important national or world issue. Always there would be a considered, intelligent and generous reply. My respect for George Will is great.

When we had our very first promotion of antique English jewelry, included in our stock were two magnificent and pricey pins – one a butterfly, the other a flower basket. A beautiful woman admired both and could not decide. In a flippant mood, Zelda said: "take both." Irene Pollin did just that. Elation! We did not realize then she was the owner of a large apartment building bearing her name, wife of the famous Abe Pollin (Capitals and Wizards, M.C.I. Center) and she also was a well-known author and philanthropist. The better we knew Irene and Abe the more we learned of and admired their dedication to civic and charitable causes.

Some years later, we secured Irene's agreement to be photographed for a full page endorsement in *Dossier* and *Washingtonian* magazines. What a hit that was! Her line was: one didn't have to go to New York to buy beautiful jewelry, now Heller was here.

Early one summer morning, just as we had opened the doors, in walked a middle-aged woman in a white tennis outfit. She was red-faced and a little sweaty – obviously just off the court. What did she want? A large yellow diamond. We were pleased to show her an 8 carat yellow diamond

Secrets of a Jeweler

in our showcase. No, she explained, that wouldn't do because she wanted LARGE. She had seen exactly what she liked in a magazine at the beauty parlor. Which salon? Which magazine? When? She didn't know.

That was our introduction to a prominent socialite, wife of the doyen of the Washington auto scene.

Some sleuthing later, we found the photograph of a humongous stone set in a pendant. We called our friend, William Goldberg, in New York. Bill was a charismatic, larger-than-life character, a de Beers sightholder and president of the Diamond Dealers Club. His inventory of large diamonds was legendary. Sure, he had just what we wanted. It would be in Chevy Chase the next morning.

There was no hesitation on the part of the handsome couple when they saw the exquisite 40 carat radiant shaped yellow diamond. They would take it at a quarter of a million. However, we would have to accent the stone with a setting of white diamonds and suspend the pendant from a customized diamond necklace. What a sale! The extras alone amounted to a sum some jewelers did not sell in the peak month of December.

This remarkable woman liked to buy her family beautiful gifts and when a new granddaughter arrived in this world, she looked at a silver and enamel Faberge frame. It was a stunning work of art in mint condition by the great Russian house, made in 1900. She found the decoration lacking, so she bought a delicate Victorian diamond pin and had us mount the pin diagonally in the upper left corner of the frame. Alas, some babies are only born with the proverbial silver spoon.

The appearance, clothing and body language of a person can often be very misleading. One can never make assumptions. Remember the scene on Rodeo Drive with Julia Roberts in *Pretty Woman*. How snooty the salespeople were, to their great loss.

On the evening of December 24th, one of the busiest times of a retailer's year, a call came from a neighboring store. Beware, the message said, there are three characters about to descend on your store. They look dangerous. We have just refused them entry. A white hippie couple and a black man. (The phone call was part of a neighborhood watch program.) We thanked them for their concern. Our policy was one of caution without discrimination. So we announced privately to our staff a 98 alert (99 would be an emergency) and admitted the three visitors.

The couple was very down to earth, exhibiting knowledge and good taste. Their companion remained quietly in attendance. They made a substantial purchase and paid with a gold card.

He introduced himself as Max Richardson. With him were his girlfriend and his driver. In conversation, Max disclosed quite modestly he was an heir to a well-known empire and he was building a collection of original Asian art.

Over the years, Max bought much beautiful jewelry from us.

Some years later Max Richardson and his girlfriend invited us to their wedding at the Women's Museum in D.C. It was a happy and magnificent celebration. The Richardsons have established an art museum in Virginia and have adopted a lovely little boy.

I teach my staff a nun in a wheelchair can hold you up and a barefoot young man in faded jeans could be a Rockefeller. Therefore reserve any hasty judgment.

Secrets of a Jeweler

*"**Heller.** It's like having the best of New York and London, right here in Chevy Chase."*

IRENE POLLIN

Irene and Abe Pollin, owners of Capital Center, the Bullets and Capitals, are acknowledged philanthropists and leaders in Washington society.

HELLER
JEWELRY · SILVER

5454 WISCONSIN AVENUE, CHEVY CHASE, MD 20815 · (301) 654-0218
10am to 5:30pm Monday through Saturday

AN IMPORTANT ENDORSEMENT

Izzy Heller

THIS ANNOUNCEMENT APPEARS AS A MATTER OF RECORD ONLY.

HELLER

announces the recent sale of the following important items:

A beautiful Diamond of high quality weighing

40 Carats

A magnificent collection of Russian Objects of Vertu by

Fabergé

HELLER
FOR FINE JEWELRY & SILVER
5454 WISCONSIN AVENUE, CHEVY CHASE, MD 20815
(301) 654-0218

TWO WEDDING RINGS

The grand opening of Heller Antiques Ltd. took place on the evening of October 28th, 1980. It was a "by invitation only" gala event. Several hundred guests attended and our little store was jam-packed. We provided valet parking. Caviar and champagne were a-plenty. We took off in style!

The very next day we had a visitor carefully examine each piece of our British antique sterling silver inventory, which at the time was either from the Georgian or Victorian periods. One could immediately see his expertise – the way he handled the pieces, looked for repairs or additions, peered at the engraving, checked the marks. He introduced himself as Charles Williams and we had a nice chat.

Charles was a good looking man of medium height with heavy spectacles, which strangely enough, he removed to examine silver close up.

He became my friend that day and remained so until his death 16 years later. We regarded him as a gentleman and a scholar.

Charles had been employed by the Department of Defense as an Army Personnel Analyst for 30 years. When we made his acquaintance, he was about to retire and devote more time to silver. He lived a few blocks from us. As a lover of fine old silver, Charles and his wife Demmy, a charming lady and a retired school teacher, had a comprehensive library, running to thousands of volumes, on antiques in general and silver in particular. Their high-ceilinged bookwall was quite magnificent. Together they frequented the auction houses and leading dealers in Washington and New York. I soon learned Charles had a great recall capability, remembering previous sales of important pieces many years earlier. He was generous with his knowledge and he became our part-time consultant and friend to me, Zelda and our staff.

It was a tradition at Heller Antiques to celebrate birthdays, anniversaries, pre-Thanksgiving, pre-New Year and anything else we could think of. Food, and in particular, chocolate cake, was always in evidence at these parties. Charles, we were convinced, could smell the cake from his house across the D.C. boundary. He would drop in and participate in the fun and our young girls in sales and gemology would enjoy his dry humor and quiet demeanor. Occasionally Demmy would accompany him.

Charles was very understated. His show of emotion to his wife was evidenced when he called Demmy "Kiddo."

He was a member of several prestigious organizations like the National Appraisers Association and the American Silver Guild, the latter which he served as President for many years. He assisted with work on the silver collections of Woodlawn Plantation and the Museum of the Daughters of the American Revolution. Charles Williams was responsible for *Silver* magazine's Q and A section.

I remember once "in the early years" when Weschler's Auctions sent me a round silver dinner plate for my comment. It had been consigned for auction as one of twelve at a high reserve and bore the perfectly struck marks of Paul Storr, a famous London silversmith. I could very soon discern it was a fake, but it was reassuring to have the confirmation of Charles Williams.

We worked together over the years on hundreds of transactions, researching, certifying, appraising. Charles felt at home in our store. We partnered some purchases. It was a friendly, relaxed association.

Charles Williams undertook a major research project for us in regard to the Davis Collection.

William True Davis was a multimillionaire businessman and also an ubiquitous figure on the Washington party circuit. He bred racehorses and drove a yellow and black Rolls Royce. In 1963 President John F. Kennedy appointed him as the American Ambassador to Switzerland where in Bern, with his wife, Virginia, he served the United States. In 1966 they undertook a safari trip to central Africa. Mrs. Davis was an expert game hunter. In Uganda, both of them were bitten by the tsetse fly and were stricken with encephalitis. She died. He recovered after months in a hospital. Back in Washington, Mr. Davis restored his life and became president of the National Bank of Washington. He began entertaining often and lavishly and as a handsome widower, he had no difficulty in always having an attractive lady at his side.

Secrets of a Jeweler

Ambassador Davis decided to dispose of his silver and invited us one evening in 1984 to visit his stone mansion on Woodland Drive to inspect his collection. Zelda and I sat in his charming wood paneled study, around a table stacked with issues of *Playboy* magazine! Within an hour we had agreed on a price and paid for the collection, which included three major items. These were:

A. a Russian Punch Bowl and Stand made in St. Petersburg, circa 1875, 36" long, weighing 1,100 ounces.

B. a pair of German sixteen-light candelabra made in Dresden, circa 1880, 38" high weighing 1,280 ounces.

C. a Victorian centerpiece with basket made in London, 1864, weighing 325 ounces engraved underneath "Breadalbane 1876"

The ambassador liked large, heavy ornate silver pieces and we were excited to acquire them.

Luckily we had brought our big Buick station wagon and that evening the ambassador, Zelda and I loaded the vehicle "to the brim" with silver treasures and in the dark offloaded them into our shop.

The next morning Charles Williams commenced his research on the Davis Collection. The primary challenge in the endeavor was the history of the sterling centerpiece. It was easy to read off the English hallmarks and to see it was made by the royal silversmith John S. Hunt. Why did it land up in Switzerland? Charles found from the armorials on the piece and from records at the Library of Congress it was a presentation piece commissioned by Queen Victoria for the retiring governor of Victoria province in Australia. The inscription refers to Breadalbane, a small town in Western Queensland. Governor Charles Joseph Latrobe returned to England where he died in 1875. His widow moved to Switzerland in 1876. Latrobe's heirs sold the centerpiece to a Swiss dealer from whom True Davis acquired it. The history was established.

We sent the centerpiece to New York, provenance and all. It did well at a public auction and it was sold to the Australian government. It is now where it belongs, in a museum "Down Under."

On Independence Day, July 4, in 1996, Charles Cecil Williams passed away at his home, survived by his wife Demmy. We miss him and will always remember him as "a gentleman and a scholar."

Some 21 ½ months later, Demmy came to my office and handed me two beautiful matching gold wedding bands – Charles' and hers – with a very touching card:

> Dear Izzy and Zelda, 18 May 1998
>
>> Please accept these and tuck them away as a memento of Charles to whom you were always so kind. I know he would be pleased. Not much intrinsic value but much sentimental value! Remember his hands (with the ring) as he examined silver.
>
> Fondly,
>
> Demmy
>
> Charles purchased the rings together. I don't want to separate them.

Zelda and I choked with emotion at the great honor bestowed upon us. The rings and the card are in our high security vault.

Secrets of a Jeweler

DEMMY AND CHARLES WILLIAMS

Izzy Heller

March 16, 2004

Dear Izzy,

Here are pictures of Charles as you knew him. I have others, perhaps, better; but they are from many years ago.

How very kind of you to include Charles in your book. I know that he considered you special. He would be pleased that you list him as important in your life.

Good luck on your project! Regards to Zelda.

Love,
Demmy

HAND WRITTEN NOTE FROM DEMMY WILLIAMS

Secrets of a Jeweler

RUSSIAN SILVER PUNCH BOWL FROM THE DAVIS COLLECTION

Izzy Heller

VICTORIAN SILVER CENTERPIECE FROM THE DAVIS COLLECTION

JUSTICE BE DONE

As you know, we Americans live in a litigious society. A man sues his neighbor, a son sues his father, Kramer sues Kramer, Erin Brockovich sues the utility and the I.R.S. sues Al Capone.

For justice to be done and to be seen to be done, we need witnesses, often experts. Expert testimony can be a very lucrative business, so I was receptive to it.

On several occasions lawyers asked me to participate as an expert in pending litigation. I had some knowledge of diamonds, jewelry and silver acquired through study, examinations, continuing education and being active in the markets here and abroad. My membership in prestigious organizations was a plus, as was the fact I possess a specialist reference library of over 600 books and articles on my subjects. I was articulate and would not be bullied in cross- examinations.

The opposing counsel initiates his contact with an expert witness by questioning credentials. Often a witness is devastated by this barrage. With the passage of time, the skin hardens and it has little impact.

My first case involved a closed circuit television deposition. The opposing attorneys, probably at $400 per hour, could not see eye-to-eye on where I should be positioned when questioned. Should the questioner also be photographed or just me? A few hours and a few thousand dollars in legal fees later, they resolved this big issue.

The divorce was ugly and there was a fight over every penny, including some everyday silver flatware.

Silver is a cheap metal, say $5 per troy ounce, as compared to gold which is say $400 per ounce. So mass-produced silver items (sterling is 92.5 percent pure) are generally worth only a small premium over the intrinsic metal. Only if there is rarity, great age and superb condition and craftsmanship will there be a great multiple of metal value – for example, when a 17th Century American dram cup weighing one ounce sells for $100,000!

The scrap over the scrap was ludicrous. The 150 pieces of sterling silver was second-hand monogrammed (a downer) 20th Century, factory-made. The net weight of sterling was perhaps 150 ounces and the value under $1,000. The legal and expert costs probably amounted to $5,000. All in the name of the theme: "I'll show my ex!" The divorce case made me feel dirty. I never testified between husband and wife again.

In 1987 a large legal group in Washington, D.C. approached me and retained me as an expert witness in a case involving the disappearance of a 3.50 carat diamond ring.

The owner of the ring was an elderly lady of modest means (let us call her Milly), whose one item of value was the ring her mother left her. Her neighbor, Betty, was her best friend. I quote from Betty's "answers to interrogators" in the case:

"I met Milly in the latter part of 1966. We became very close in the last eight years – like sisters. We visited each other several times a week, and would talk every day either on the phone or in person.

Milly was receiving $250 a month in alimony payments; her social security was $389 and she had a small income from employment. She had modest furnishings, a fur coat and the 3.50 carat solitaire diamond ring which the defendant (the apartment manager) obtained either from Milly for safekeeping or from Milly's apartment after her death. I saw the ring on several occasions. She kept it in a little white cardboard box, together with 2 platinum wedding bands all held together with a large safety pin. Milly would wear the ring on special occasions, like when she went to a party at Easter time at the Smiths.

After Milly was admitted to the hospital on an emergency basis, I checked her apartment (at her request) to make sure the ring was safe and found it in the same box fastened together as stated before.

I saw the 3 rings for the last time the day after Milly came back from the hospital, which was 2 days before her passing.

On the afternoon of Milly's death, I entered her apartment and found that her desk, which was always closed, was open and the key, normally under the clock, was missing.

Secrets of a Jeweler

When confronted, the apartment manager who was the only person other than me who had legal access to Milly's apartment, told me the diamond rings were given to her for safekeeping and the rings were a matter only between Milly and her.

I told the manager that Milly's will, a copy of which Milly gave me on my birthday, December 9th in 1985, left me specifically the 3 rings and generally all the remaining contents of the flat.

The manager, a few days later, reluctantly agreed to hand over the rings to me. I looked at the big ring and immediately spotted the difference. The prongs of the solitaire looked beaten up. I looked at the stone. It lacked the sparkle and sharpness of Milly's diamond. I told the manager the stone had been switched. She denied any wrongdoing. I then took the ring to Intercontinental Jewelers on New Hampshire Avenue, and they confirmed the center stone was a fake, a $20 cubic zirconium."

That was the statement of Betty, the deceased's neighbor. Her lawyer advised her to sue the owners and managing agents of the apartment complex as well as the individual defendant who served as resident manager.

The amount of the claim revolved primarily round the value of the 3.50 carat round diamond. An appraisal dated 1956 by Macy's, New York described the stone as "modern cut, white, with no imperfection discernible."

Today's gemologists would dismiss an appraisal with that description as hopeless. "Modern cut" presumably referred to a round brilliant with 58 facets – but what were the measurements, the percentages of table and depth to girdle, what were the polish and symmetry like, the girdle, the fluorescence? The difference between a stone with a good make and a mediocre make could account for a 40 percent difference in value.

As to color, the best is colorless, an absence of color. Is this what Macy's meant when they wrote "white." And how colorless? There are three grades of colorless diamonds with letters of the alphabet: D, E and F. Values differ for each grade.

The supreme clarity grade is flawless. Flawless even under microscopic examination. The appraisal referred to "no imperfection discernible." Was this to the naked eye (possibly a SI2 grade) or when viewed through a loupe (internally flawless)? The difference in price is enormous. We were faced with a range of value from $10,000 to $60,000 for the 3.50 carat diamond – depending on whose side you were on. I acted for the building owners, who wanted the lowest possible value.

Luckily the matter was settled an hour before going to trial, and I was not called to testify. I was quite relieved and went home with a check for my availability. Hopefully, justice was done.

THE WHITE HOUSE

Until a decade ago, the old-established firm of C.J. Vander Limited of London, England was owned by the Vander family, a major supplier to us of fine antique and modern silverware.

A tour of their premises near the Silver Vaults was always rewarding. Their inventory was spectacular in quantity and quality. In their workshops, one could see flatware (knives, forks and spoons) being made by hand the same way it had been a century earlier. In one room, I saw a custom piece in progress for the Sultan of Brunei – a sterling silver mosque to be fitted in the Sultan's jumbo jet.

Over the years, customers would frequently ask us for a unique presentation piece in silver and we decided a paperweight of the White House was the answer. We commissioned C.J. Vander to manufacture such an item for us.

They needed photographs of the President's residence, not only in elevation, but also of the roof. While I was reading Vander's letter, a young man by the name of Leonard entered my office asking for work. He was a photographer just starting out. "Give me my first break," he pleaded. I gave him the job of taking photos of 1600 Pennsylvania Avenue.

A few days later, I took a call from a Secret Service agent advising he had taken a young man into custody after suspicious behavior on a tall ladder near the fence of the White House. I assured the agent Leonard was harmless and was on assignment for me to "shoot" the White House for the purpose of making a paperweight. He was not impressed with my answer, but released our photographer.

We made 500 beautiful replicas of the White House. The onyx bases allowed for applying engraved silver inscriptions. We had special fitted boxes for the paperweights. They sold like the proverbial hotcakes at $385 each.

I think Leonard would have had a much harder time with the authorities guarding the White House if he had secured his first break, post 9-11.

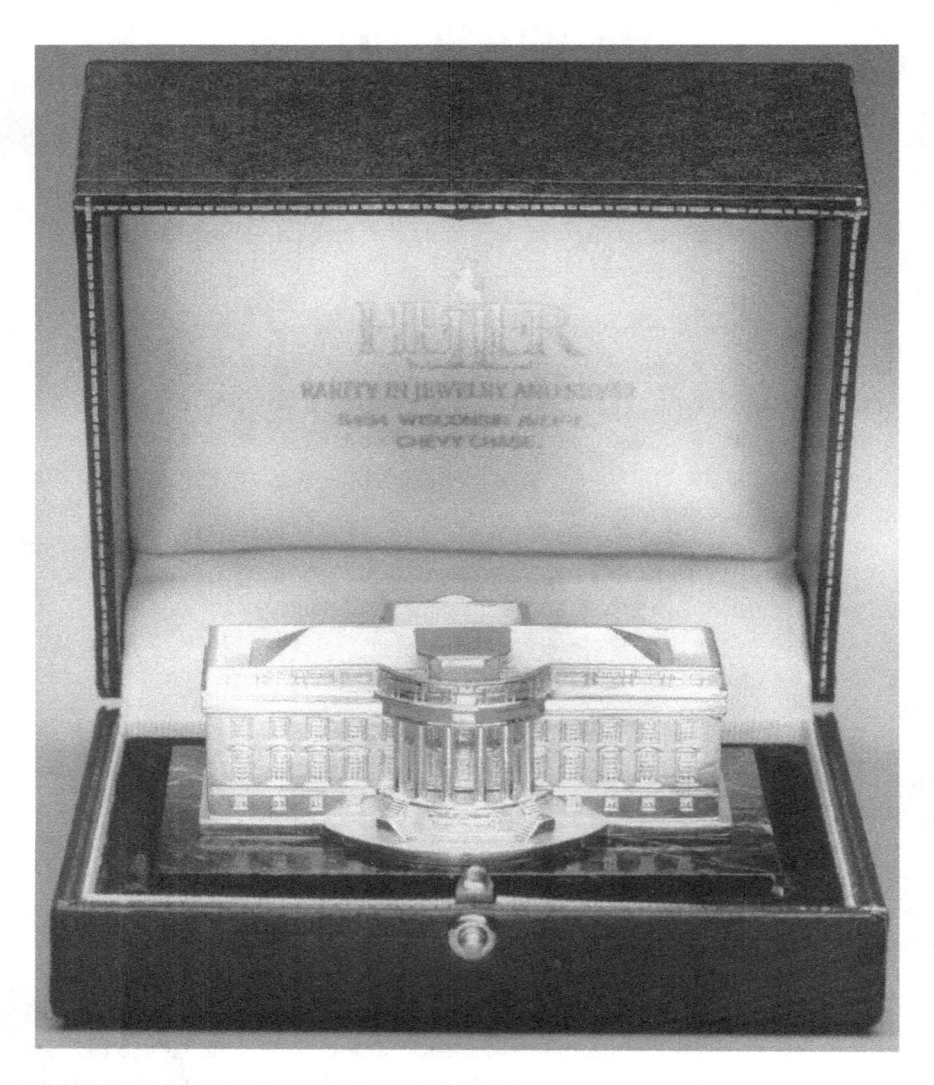

BOXED SILVER PAPERWEIGHT DEPICTING THE WHITE HOUSE

HIS EXCELLENCY OUT OF AFRICA

Since the end of World War II, the map of Africa has been redrawn and re-colored many times. British, French, Portuguese and Belgian territories have gained independence and been renamed. These changes have generally not brought the promised peace and prosperity.

West Africa is home to some of the poorest people on the continent, despite adequate resources of agricultural soil and mineral wealth.

In one such country, which we shall call Boureaux, the ruler took thousands of political prisoners and was responsible for the exile of hundreds of thousands of the population. Because of his reign of terror, agriculture was devastated and famine was widespread. A bloody coup by the military ended the strong man's rule. Colonel Kalo became the new dictator in 1985.

Boureaux had a diamond mine and Kalo was determined to sell its output. With this in mind, he sent 50,000 carats (equal to 10,000 grams or 22 pounds) of rough diamond crystals (unpolished stones) to the largest consuming market in the world, the U.S.A. – more particularly to his Ambassador, whose embassy was in a townhouse near Massachusetts Avenue, N.W., in Washington, DC.

Ambassador Ansa wasted no time and soon sold the entire parcel of diamonds to a local man, Abdul Mohammed for the enormous sum of $2.5 million, payable immediately.

Despite so-called guarantees, Mohammed's check bounced and the Ambassador, fearing for his life, called in the F.B.I.

Soon thereafter, the thief was arrested and most of the diamonds were recovered and held by the authorities until the trial was over.

The prestigious law firm whose client was the country of Boureaux, had not been paid for their services for this and other legal matters, and therefore had a lien on the diamonds.

My good friend and client, attorney Stevens, was the partner dealing with Boureaux's account. It was now his job to dispose of the stones. Stevens called the only person he knew in the diamond business and asked if I wanted to buy 45,000 carats of diamonds.

I was stunned and all ears when I heard what had transpired. What an opportunity had come my way!

Soon, I put together a partnership of experts from New York and one early morning we met in the basement of Riggs Bank across from the White House. Present at the meeting were His Excellency Ambassador Ansa and his charges d'affaires, who sat on one side of a large rectangular table and on the other side my two partners and me. There was one other at the table, Stevens' assistant, attorney Alice, who acted as the French-English translator, since we were told the two men from Boureaux only spoke French.

Eighty percent of the lot consisted of melee which are tiny diamonds, thirty points and under (100 points = 1 carat). The rest ranged in size up to 15 carats per stone, with some outstanding colorless and bright yellow diamonds. My job was to open and weigh the evidence: the plastic bags of diamonds sealed by the F.B.I. one by one, and pass it to partner A, the technical expert, who evaluated it for recutting potential in the case of the larger stones. Partner B, the commercial specialist, established prices per carat for each group.

After four hours of tense concentrated effort on our part with little said or done by the French side, we were ready to make our offer backed by a Riggs Bank letter of credit. We asked Alice to convey to the representatives of Boureaux we were ready.

Before we could present our bid however, an unexpected turn of events occurred. The charges d' affaires beckoned to me and to my shock said in good English: "Mr. Heller, I need to talk to you in private."

We got up from the table and went to an adjoining office. Ansa informed me he had put in an inordinate amount of time in this matter and needed to be compensated. "What does that mean?" I asked. "Each of us requires $100,000 in U.S. bills," he replied.

I knew immediately my participation in the purchase was over. However, I politely responded by saying I would confer with my partners. The New Yorkers were 100 percent behind me in saying they would not be buyers under such a condition. This demand was a deal-breaker.

Several weeks later I received the following very polite letter from Ansa:

Dear Mr. Heller:

> I have been informed that my government has chosen a purchaser among those who have been doing business in Boureaux and, therefore, have deposited currency with our Central Bank.
>
> I hope you will be able to negotiate the purchase of other diamonds with my government in the future.
>
> Please accept, with my best wishes for the New Year, the assurance of my kindest consideration. signed

Ambassador Ansa

That was the official and diplomatic letter of closure. My friend attorney Stevens disclosed details of the actual follow-up. A Lebanese buyer had appeared on the scene and bought the entire parcel of diamonds for $2.7 million. On that basis, the gentleman from Beirut could live in luxury for the rest of his days.

The poor people of Boureaux battle on . . . .

OUR FRIEND, LENA

In my childhood, I would not dare to admire a woman of color in public. That was South Africa at the time. Indeed, it was surprising such a female would be featured in film on the bioscope, as the cinema was known.

But there she was, Lena Horne, a magnificent, vivacious singer activating the hormones of our teenage group as we sat in the darkness of the Scala Theatre on High Street, Worcester, South Africa.

In my wildest dreams, I could never have imagined this beauty would become my friend years later in a place 3,000 miles away. Life is strange.

So, as chance would have it, decades later, Sherman Sneed, Lena's manager and companion, would step out of the limousine with the great film star to grace the little establishment known as Heller Jewelers.

Lena wore dark glasses, said little. When she did speak it was softly and with a hint of laughter in her voice. She was magnificent. All business, however, was conducted by the charming, efficient Sherman.

She liked earrings and big rings. Diamonds. And we were happy to oblige her.

Lena had taken up residence on Connecticut Avenue in Washington, D.C. and become a regular and V.I.P. client. Like many such customers, she became our friend. So much so, she invited us to two fabulous functions.

The first was the Kennedy Center Honors in 1984 where she, and four others (Danny Kaye, Gian Carlo Menotti, Arthur Miller and Isaac Stern) were lauded by the U.S. President and a distinguished audience. What an evening!

After the awards ceremony, Lena invited Zelda and me to a private dinner party. There were four tables of eight guests each. I was seated next to a most interesting couple, he a publisher of fiction from New York.

(Someone once said the difference between an editor and a publisher is this: An editor selects manuscripts while a publisher selects editors!)

I was quick to tell my dinner companion about my endeavor to write a work of "faction" (historical fiction) about my life in South Africa and that I had completed some 90 pages of the novel. Would he review my amateurish effort? He graciously acceded.

I sent him my manuscript and two months later, I got a detailed "crit" which was overall complimentary.

With the help of Zelda and a friend, Janice Blumberg, I finished the book *Deadly Truth*. Were it not for that chance meeting, the 90 pages would have been left intact to collect dust.

The other fab function was Lena's concert at the Warner Theatre in downtown Washington, where we were given front row seats. Lena ordered a large diamond ring, which involved intricate design and required much craftsmanship. She specified the ring had to be ready for opening night. What a rush! Well, the ring was completed just in time and we delivered it backstage to Sherman half an hour before the curtain went up.

Lena came onstage to the deafening applause of the audience, spotted us in the front row, pointed to her dazzling ring and blew us a kiss. We were blown over. The soft spoken lady in our store became the talented powerful performer, belting out *The Lady is a Tramp* and other of her trademark songs. The audience was wowed. Standing ovations! Screams of delight! She hypnotized all of us. That magical night, every one of us fell in love with Lena Horne.

In the early days, Lena was referred to as a "chocolate chanteuse" and danced in the chorus at Harlem's famous Cotton Club, where blacks entertained a strictly white clientele. She encountered horrible racism in her life so it is not surprising she devoted much time to the civil rights movement in the 1960's.

Lena became an international star of stage and screen, playing with such giants as Judy Garland, Bing Crosby and Frank Sinatra.

She told us she was very proud of the honorary doctorate she received from Howard University in D.C. a few years before we met her. "I had been offered doctorates earlier," she said, "and had turned them down because I hadn't earned them at college. But when Howard presented the honor to me, I knew I had graduated from the school of life, and so I accepted it."

THE SHERATON SYSTEM

Before the advent of the Jacob Javitz Exhibition Center in Manhattan, the bi-annual Jewelers of America Shows were accommodated in two large hotels – The Sheraton and the Hilton, located just a few blocks from each other in midtown Manhattan.

Thousands of jewelers from the 50 states and abroad attended these events causing major congestion at the hotel check-in counters, the elevators, the meeting rooms, and the ballrooms. Delays and confusion and the concomitant thieving would inevitably be present at the shows.

Despite these frustrations, Zelda and I would attend and later exhibit at these exciting conventions. Because New York has a very strong trade union culture, we found we had to use expensive unionized labor for many tasks. On one occasion, when we checked out at the Sheraton after an exhausting show, we found we needed three specialists – a bellman, a hall porter, and a curbside scheduler – to move our luggage from our room to the cab. Three tips, a change of carts and a damn nuisance, to say the least.

At that time, we shipped all our inventory back home fully insured for millions of dollars by Brinks Armored, who had a booth in the Sheraton's ballroom for convenience and safety.

That is, all our inventory, except for one fabulous South Sea Pearl necklace. The matching pearls were spherical, unblemished and lustrously cream. The graduation of diameters was from 14.5 to 17 millimeters. Big bucks. $110,000 to be exact. I bought it at the last minute after we closed our Brinks shipment. Because I negotiated a big discount and didn't want to face the possibility of substitution of the prized pearls, I decided I would assume the risk and take it in my briefcase on the flight to National Airport, Washington, D.C.

Zelda and I paid our hotel bill, and had the bellman load two large suitcases and one small suitcase on to his cart. When he lifted the small case, he commented on its heaviness. Books and advertising material which I assembled from various booths accounted for the weight. The bellman may have thought it was heavy because of gold jewelry.

We accompanied the man down the elevator to the lobby, I clutching my briefcase with the six-figure pearls. There, after a short interval, we transferred to the hall porter.

Finally we were at the curbside, in line for our taxi to La Guardia airport.

The curbside scheduler was the best-dressed of the three Sheraton bag handlers. He had a fancy uniform, complete with shiny buttons, braided epaulets and a hat, which could have outshone that of a marching bandleader.

When our cab pulled up, Mr. Fancy Hat placed our two large suitcases in the trunk and slammed it shut. Simultaneously I saw a man grab our small case and run to the subway entrance, half a block from us. Had he been tipped off about the heaviness?

Zelda was shocked and furious. She was ready to chase the thief. I restrained and pacified her.

I calmed myself with the thought what the thief stolen had no commercial value. And I imagined him unzipping the bag to find the heavy books stuffed around the edges with my dirty socks.

I got into the taxi, opened my briefcase and smiled at the exquisite necklace of rare South Sea Pearls.

They glowed back.

QE2

I was becoming a popular lecturer at Rotary, Kiwanis, Oasis, International Society of Appraisers and at church and synagogue groups.

My audiences were always quiet and attentive, that is except for one occasion when an elderly lady in the front row of the hall disturbed me with her non-stop chattering to her neighbor. Although I heard only complimentary remarks from her, I could not concentrate on my talk. Eventually I stopped, looked her straight in the eye and said: "Mother, behave yourself!"

In 1986, the Expert Lecturers' Service of New Jersey heard of us and invited Zelda and me to be the guests of the Cunard Line on a transatlantic voyage on board the Queen Elizabeth 2, at the time one of the largest and finest cruise ships in the world, sailing from New York to Southampton, England. They asked for two one-hour lectures on jewelry and silver. We didn't take long to respond affirmatively.

Some months later we embarked at Manhattan's new passenger ship terminal located at 50th Street and the Hudson River, the farthest west you can go in the city. There, waiting for us and our fellow passengers, were porters to take our bags. Stewardesses escorted us to our seats alongside the ship for champagne, afternoon tea and English sandwiches while the QE 2's band played upbeat music. This certainly set the tone. When we walked up the ramp and had our photographs taken, we were all hyped up for a super vacation.

The statistics of the QE 2 are awesome. Tonnage over 67,000. Length just short of 1,000 feet. Speed 30 knots.

As it turned out, the sea was calm, the cruise was magnificent. With a time adjustment of one hour a day, there was no such thing as jet lag. Three days out in mid-ocean, the captain announced a minor problem with an engine which would require rectification with the ship coming to a dead halt. The passengers cheered. We felt we were in a magnificent palace getting royal treatment with exciting entertainment all day and all night. The extra day at sea was welcomed by all, except perhaps the crew.

The food choices were staggering and the wine cellar even had wines from my home town in South Africa.

Harrods, that wonderful London store, had a well-stocked branch on the ship and Zelda had a great shopping spree when she tired of the casino.

One evening my wife announced at dinner she felt she was going to be a winner that night at the final Bingo Game of the cruise. Quite a large jackpot had accumulated. She played the five games and lost each time. Where was her winning streak?, I teased. And then the Cruise Director asked for all the losing tickets to be put in a large bowl. Zelda won the grand prize of $1,000, which she graciously shared amongst the five couples at our dinner table.

Robert Vaughn, the movie star, who acted in the thriller *Bullit* with Steve McQueen, was also invited as a guest lecturer. He introduced that film when it was screened on board.

Also doing his thing was invitee Dr. Murray Banks, author of *What To Do Until the Psychiatrist Comes!* who left us with a head-full of ideas and a belly-full of laughs.

There were other lecturers dealing with health, finance and history. We were in happy company and had a lot of fun with our colleagues.

The response to our lectures was great. Several passengers gave us orders for large diamonds and one bought a Georgian flatware set with green ivory knife handles.

A few months later, Cunard offered us a 91-day round-the-world cruise on a similar arrangement but we could not absent ourselves for that long a time.

Seventeen years later, however, we repeated "the crossing of the pond" and again enjoyed the old-world majesty of the QE 2. This time there was far more security and we paid our way.

Secrets of a Jeweler

QUEEN ELIZABETH 2

Izzy Heller

DAILY · PROGRAMME

GOOD MORNING - TODAY IS THURSDAY 12TH JUNE

8.00	**The Lindsay Frost Breakfast Show**	Radio Channel 1
	Music, comment, the latest weather conditions and surprise guests — The fun way to wake up!!!	
9.00	**QE2 Scavenger Hunt** - Entry Forms are available from the Cruise Staff Office. A prize will be awarded for the first correct or nearest correct solution handed into the Cruise Staff Office before 3.00 p.m. today	
9.00	**Today's Brain Teaser: "Showbiz" Quiz** is available from the Library. A prize will be awarded for the first correct or nearest correct solution handed in to your QE2 Librarian, Eleanor Smith, before 3.00 p.m. today. The winning entry will be posted outside the Library at 5.00 p.m. today, together with the correct answers so you can check how well you did in today's Quiz.	
9.30	**Bridge Lecture** with Ed Lewis	Double Room
9.30	**Cruise Sales Manager Ted Eastwick** is available daily on 2 Deck by G Stairway from 9.30 a.m. to 12 Noon and from 3.00 p.m. to 5.00 p.m. for information and advance bookings on all Cunard/NAC ships. Holiday and Winter Cruises aboard Sagafjord & Vistafjord are already booking heavily, so stop by today. Your Travel Agent receives full credit	
9.30	**Opera Music for Opera Lovers**	Radio Channel 3
	Tapes kindly lent to QE2 by the Metropolitan Opera Guild in celebration of the Guild's 50th Anniversary. Today's programme features 'Der Ring Des Niblungen' by Wagner and 'La Boheme' by Puccini	
10.00	**Computer Seminar: Computers in Your Pocket**	Computer Learning Centre
	(Portable Computers) with Bill Voss, QE2's Computer Lecturer	
10.30	**Morning Video: "The Queen Mary"**	Double Down Bar Aft
	In May 1986 the Queen Mary celebrated her 50th anniversary of her maiden voyage. This video presentation features actual footage of the maiden voyage, together with shots of her home in Long Beach, California. (This video will be repeated at 11.00 a.m.)	
10.30	**QE2 Quiz** - Test your knowledge of the greatest ship in the world with members of the Cruise Staff	Double Room
10.30	**'SILVER FOR THE COLLECTOR"** An informal talk, illustrated with slides, by **ZELDA & ISRAEL HELLER**, Gemologists and experts in antique silver and jewellery through the ages	Theatre

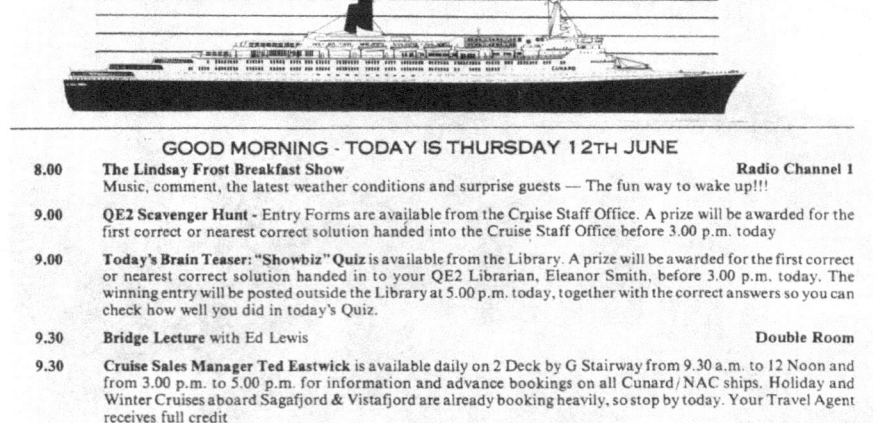

PROGRAMME INDICATING OUR TALK AT 10:30AM

Secrets of a Jeweler

ZELDA WITH MOVIE STAR, ROBERT VAUGHN

$3.25 MILLION

Many years ago, in an effort to promote ourselves as diamond experts, we took over a vacant store alongside our own in the Barlow Building for a week and set up a diamond factory complete with wheel and cutter to demonstrate polishing. Hundreds of people visited daily and all were fascinated by the live show and our videos, educational literature and lectures. On display were rare stones including large natural color yellow and pink diamonds.

We also had a $3.25 million necklace, courtesy of Bill Goldberg, the prominent diamond sightholder from New York who agreed to participate in our show.

In addition to other security personnel, we hired an off-duty armed police officer to protect Zelda who wore the necklace. Each of the diamonds was D in color and Flawless in clarity. The total weight of the fabulous stones came to 127 carats.

We believe the necklace was sold to a Saudi Prince, but we will never know because the transaction was handled secretly by an intermediary.

William Goldberg was known for the magic he brought to diamonds. This family-run business – now with Saul, Deborah, Barry and Eve - boasts more than 50 years of passion and commitment to the finest diamonds in the world.

Bill had the courage to bet on beauty. Some of the famous stones that passed his way are:

- "Rough Pink" – 40.34 carat
- "Premier Rose" – 137 carat pear shape
- "Guinea Star" – 84 carat oval shape
- "Vivid Pink Muse" – 8.9 carat oval shape
- "Blue Lili" – 30 carat trapezoid shape (named for his wife)

- "Red Shield" – 5 carat shield shape – worlds largest fancy red at the time

- "Briolette" – 75 carat briolette shape

- "The Pumpkin" – 5.54 carat (fancy vivid orange)

- "Belluga" – 102 carat oval shape – largest D Flawless oval in history

The story of the Premier Rose is as extraordinary as the stone itself. Plucked from a conveyor belt by an alert miner, the rough stone weighed 354 carats – an almost inconceivable find at South Africa's Premier Mine, which rarely produces gem diamonds in large sizes. After making sixty trial runs to see how the stone could be cut, a daring decision was made at William Goldberg. The stone would be sawn against the grain. Months of sawing, cutting and polishing yielded three diamonds. The magnificent pear shape 137 carat Premier Rose, certified as a D flawless. The Little Rose, a beautiful 31 carat pear shape diamond. And the Baby Rose, a 2 carat brilliant.

Personalities like Sophia Loren and Sharon Stone have modeled Goldberg diamonds.

With the sponsorship of the great William Goldberg, our promotion did well. Sales were brisk and far exceeded expectations. The public and the media raved about our successful exhibition and we steered our business into the world of diamonds.

Izzy Heller

THE GREAT WILLIAM GOLDBERG

Secrets of a Jeweler

ZELDA WEARING THE EXQUISITE NECKLACE

CUSTOMERS WHO STEAL

Confusion and Distraction are two of the many tricks used by jewelry thieves.

Ralph, my brother in London, tells how a group of gypsies would use a child as distraction. A couple would cut their child's finger, squeeze out the blood and loudly blame the sharp edge on a cabinet or a chair for the injury. Meanwhile as everyone's focus was on the poor kid, another member of the team was jimmying open a case and filling his bag.

Mice have been released, old ladies have fainted – all to distract, confuse and steal. Who said thieves were fools?

At one of our Sunday promotions, a charming young man engaged my wife in an interesting conversation. He was Billy Joel's manager – so he said – and wanted something special to soothe his long-suffering wife who had to put up with his constant traveling. A large Kashmir sapphire ring was his final choice at $14,000. He was at the Madison Hotel (we could and did verify this) and he would send us a check the next day.

No check came by Wednesday. He had left the hotel. The police said that 5 other stores had been sold "the same bill of goods" that Sunday. My wife was asked for a description of the man. She froze and could contribute little.

Our good friend, Dr. Sidney Fogelman, whose wife, Sylvia, was a sales colleague, offered to take photographs at our show and a week later he presented us with the prints. Included were front and side views of the charming Mr. Billy Joel's manager. He was I.D.'d by the police and arrested soon after. We never recovered the ring or received any payment.

A well-known furrier called me one day to ask if I could purchase a large collection of designer jewelry. A woman had run up a sizable account with him and also at Neiman Marcus and was embarrassed because the stock market had collapsed and her broker made a call for funds. She was prepared to sell her excess jewelry.

Secrets of a Jeweler

The excess amounted to $150,000 and I was pleased to pay for signed, saleable "goods."

We photographed, gem tested, measured, entered, priced and tagged the items and now the sales associate was to display them. The rule, which was frequently broken, was to keep the showcases locked at all times. In the short span of turning her back on an unlocked case, a heavy Henry Dunay cuff bangle was snitched. At first, we were so naïve. It had to be there somewhere. No one could have stolen it. The playback of the videotape told us differently. There we saw the customer lean over, grab and drop. All in milliseconds. Goodbye three grand!

A person walked into our store and seemed more interested in the overhead lights than our merchandise. I was suspicious of the man right from the start and warned Chris with our secret 98 code. She nodded that she understood. Her caution was no match for his slight of hand and a man's diamond ring was found absent from the tray after he left.

Two other of the many instances of traceable theft are of the *Chutzpah* variety, what we call The Mouth and The Elastic Band.

Our insurance company sends us regular bulletins informing us of their loss experiences. Watch out for someone who keeps looking up and down the walls and ceiling. He's probably casing the joint. Or for someone who quickly looks at this and that and asks for more and more to be shown.

The latter behavior was what alerted our bookkeeper, Jennifer, to keep an eye on him through her one-way mirror. It was just as well because the salesperson was in total confusion. And through the glass, Jennifer saw him put something in his mouth. She pressed the panic button without hesitation.

The thief ambled to the exit but Jennifer hopped out of her cubicle and engaged him in small talk. When he attempted to leave, the locked door would not open. All our staff had been alerted not to engage the exit mechanism.

A Bethesda police officer arrived within minutes and forced the man to open his mouth. The officer remove a diamond pin complete with our two tags. "I don't know how it could have got there," was all he could say as they cuffed him.

The other chutzpah incident involved a customer who requested a stunning diamond bracelet. We had many. After numerous questions and much discussion, he selected one. He asked whether we had a nice velvet box. "Yes," the sales associate replied. He continued: "Let me see it . . . O.K." He peered down at the bracelet in the long velvet box. "Yes. But do you take American Express? I want the miles," he said. We confirmed acceptance. "Hold this for a few moments. I'll get my card from the car," he asked. He left, never to be seen again. The velvet box was empty. The bird had flown with a $22,000 diamond beauty.

The police told us they knew of this perpetrator. His "modus operandi" was to attach the jewelry item to a hook at the end of an elastic band attached to the inside of his sleeve.

The thief was skilled at slight of hand. He hoodwinked us completely.

Secrets of a Jeweler

SIDNEY AND SYLVIA FOGELMAN WITH ZELDA AND IZZY

THE GRAVY TRAIN

The American Silver Guild is an association based in the Washington metro area whose members meet about 10 times annually, sometimes in private homes to socialize and discuss silver.

Through my membership of the A.S.G., I have met many serious collectors. Someone once said, one out of three Americans is a collector and one out of three is eccentric. I don't know if this means one out of three collectors is eccentric!

Mr. and Mrs. Judson C. French are long time members of the Guild and are ardent students and collectors of Argyles.

Jud French is a world-renown scientist and was the Director of the Electronics and Electrical Engineering Laboratory at NIST, formerly the National Bureau of Standards. In the 1960's he and other scientists developed measurement methods for semiconductors that became fundamental to computers, cell phones and most electronics. Judy is a vivacious person, formerly a photo librarian for The National Geographic Society. She is an authority and lectures on pre-Columbian history, Japanese culture, horticulture, and environmental issues. They are a delightful couple.

Let me tell you an Argyle (sometimes spelled Argyll) is a heat retaining gravy pitcher, generally called a gravy warmer.

Since the early 1700's the English have carved and served their meat at the table. The customary gravy server was the open boat-shaped vessel. Unfortunately, while the host carved, the gravy cooled.

To rectify this irritant, one of the Scottish Dukes of Argyle got his silversmith to make a few gravy warmers. Thereafter, heat-retaining "gravy pots" of that design bore the Duke's name. Argyles are almost exclusively British.

The designs of the heating mechanism were mainly one of two simple systems: a central cylinder to house a heated iron rod or a central cylinder, a separate bottom or an outer jacket which was filled with hot water.

Thanks to the generosity of an anonymous donor, the Portland Art Museum in Oregon, has 33 argyles – what may be one of the largest and most complete collections of silver argyles in the public domain.

Because of my friendship with Judy and Jud French and their enthusiasm for Argyles, I contacted every source at my disposal with the request to be on the lookout for gravy warmers. One cold morning at 5 a.m. in London at the Bermondsey Market, I picked up one. In South Africa, another. In Toronto and New York more. Over a period of 20 years, perhaps 10 in total, each magnificently different.

Having regard to the rarity of Argyles, the Frenchs', with my help, built an impressive collection of fine quality specimens.

Some years ago, I hosted a meeting of the A.S.G. in my store. Twenty-two of the French collection Argyles were on display. Mrs. French gave a lecture on Argyles and discussed each of her babies in great detail.

Jud and Judy were so scholarly and discriminating in their decisions – real connoisseurs.

It was a pleasure to participate in the process and be with them on the gravy train.

Izzy Heller

JUDSON AND JUDY FRENCH WITH IZZY

Secrets of a Jeweler

A SHEFFIELD PLATE ARGYLE

Izzy Heller

A STERLING SILVER ARGYLE

THE BOUCHERON BRACELET

They were an elderly well-groomed couple, childless, recently retired and still very much in love. They had not lost their English accents although they had lived in the States for over 50 years.

It is great to converse with cultured people who have a nice sense of humor. That was the case with the Lawrences, who would visit regularly and pick up some small trinkets.

On one such visit in 1986, I admired a large and stunning multicolored bracelet she was wearing. I asked if I could examine it. She removed it from her wrist and handed to me.

What I saw was a wide gold braided strap with curved links. I turned it over and marveled at its intricacy. The colored stones enhancing the diamonds were the big three (emeralds, rubies and sapphires) and also what some refer to as "semi-precious," namely, amethysts. I had never seen a more beautiful bracelet. Here was genius of design and craftsmanship. I told her so. And added "I'd love to buy it."

"It's not for sale, at any price." Mrs. L replied. "My husband gave it to me six months after the end of World War II while we were visiting Paris. I adore my Boucheron," she firmly declared.

The years went by. Mr. L died. Mrs. L was frail and had hefty expenses. She made an appointment to see me.

She opened the original fitted box and I marveled once again at the sight of the exquisite bracelet. I had to have it, I decided.

"Let's be clear on one thing. I'm not giving it away. You said you'd like to buy it and if you can pay my price it's yours. And my price is $50,000."

I handed the piece to Zelda, who is a graduate gemologist and asked her to check the piece for breakdown value. I knew whatever figure she came up with would be irrelevant. It was more to buy time.

The asking price by usual standards was outrageous. And when Zelda produced a tabulation reflecting the values of 60 grams of 18 karat gold, the diamonds, the colored stones, her total was some $5,600. Even factoring in the artistic beauty and the signature of a great French jeweler, in no way could the $50,000 be justified.

The heart won over the mind and I made out the check. Mrs. L was gracious. She was sorry to part with her treasure, yet she knew the time had come. She hoped it went to a good home.

Zelda thought I had gone nuts. How could I have paid such an enormous price, beauty or not. We would never recover our investment!

We priced the bracelet at $69,000 and hoped. It looked gorgeous in the showcase. Everything else on the trays looked passé.

From time to time, dealers from New York would pop in and scout our inventory. Monroe was one such. When he saw the Boucheron, he could hardly contain himself. Daddy had taught him not to show joyous emotion but he failed the instruction. He, like me, had to be the custodian of the bracelet. After a hell of a haggle, he bought it for $55,000.

I took his check and waved it at Zelda. "You see," I gloated. But that is not the end of my story.

Several months later, Monroe was on the phone. "You remember the Boucheron bracelet." As if I'd forget. "I handed it to Sotheby's at a reserve of $50,000 in the hope that it will take off. They promised me a free color illustration."

Item #512 devoted one full page to a full color picture of the masterpiece and another page to a description of the piece (estimate $55,000 to $65,000) with a blurb on the House of Boucheron which read as follows:

In 1858, Frederic Boucheron (1830-1902) opened a small shop in the Palais Royale section of Paris. His success was such that, by 1893, he moved to a mansion in the Place Vendome, thus becoming first in a series of jewelers to occupy this now famous area. The new premises was formerly the private residence of the Countess de Castiglione, a famous society beauty of the Second Empire.

In 1931, Louis Boucheron, son of the founder, was chosen by the Shah of Iran to evaluate and catalogue his vast treasury of jewels and was designated official curator of the collection by imperial decree.

With branches throughout the world, Boucheron today continues to serve as jeweler to an elite group of international clients. The firm remains in family hands under the direction of Alain Boucheron, great-grandson of the founder.

The hammer knocked down the bid of $130,000, which made the cost of the bracelet to Sotheby's buyer (10 percent premium) a whopping $143,000.

This was vindication at its best. I reminded Zelda of her comment that I was nuts. Her response was "If you knew it was so valuable, why did you sell it for $55,000?"

Monroe showed his gratitude by sending us a basket of fruit.

Izzy Heller

THE BOUCHERON BRACELET

DAN, DAN THE LADIES MAN

Daniel Bloom was married, played tennis five times weekly, each time followed by a massage, had homes in D.C., New York and London, had three girl friends and was a remarkable 87 years of age!

Tall and dapper, if a little weather-beaten, Dan grew up as an orphan. He was lucky to get a Harvard education and a legal position in the White House.

He had street-smarts and a nose for money. By the time he was thirty he had made his first million. Ten years later, he was in the ten million league.

He built up a chain of loan institutions in Texas, which he directed from afar. His wife was the president of his financial empire. He would see her two or three times a year, on each occasion for a day or two. It was too complicated and too costly to divorce her. He employed a private eye to monitor her activities and was furious to learn she had a lover. Not so much she took a man to her bed, but he was a no-goodnik.

Dan was an impeccable dresser. His good taste and style extended beyond clothes and women to jewelry. And that's how I met this character.

Dan's mistresses were not dumb blondes. Or rather they were not dumb. Each was blonde, in her forties, a divorcee, successful in a profession, well built and pretty.

Dan became an important client who was building a collection of fine jewelry for an investment, an item of diversification in his large portfolio.

He brought Lily, the architect, with him to select a necklace. She had a vivacious personality. They were in my office looking at some alternatives when Dan said: "You have the wrong neckline to model these." She rectified the matter by removing her high-necked sweater to reveal a lacy delicate bra. He winked at me proudly and bought her the most expensive necklace. Shortly after the purchase, Dan and Lily went yachting in the Caribbean. He showed me the photos of himself kayaking. Lily had taught him. She was a great teacher.

Dan invested with Frances, a merchant banker, and had done well by her. She was much more reserved than Lily. She showed far less emotion when he bought her the large catseye chrysoberyl ring. It had to be sized and was going to be presented at Matisse restaurant on Wisconsin Avenue, D.C. the following night. Zelda and I arrived at Matisse at the arranged time to find Frances already seated. No Dan. He was ill she said, and when he had a cold he was miserable. Dilemma! I had the ring in my pocket. The plan was Dan would put it on her finger before dessert was served. Frances read my mind and assured me that it was okay to give her the ring, which I did before the appetizers.

Jennifer was my favorite of the three. She was chancellor of a large university in Oklahoma and a real lady. She applied for the top job in a national non-profit in D.C., where Dan was on the board. She didn't get the position, but Dan got her.

Dan went to New York periodically for board meetings of a public company. Jennifer and he were together in his Park Avenue penthouse one week when Zelda and I were in Manhattan on business. We decided to meet for dinner at my favorite midtown restaurant, The Red Eye Grill.

The four of us sat talking for an hour after the meal had been enjoyed. We always had a lot to discuss with Dan, who was a bit of a know-all, but interesting nonetheless. Jennifer was no push-over and had her own ideas on many issues.

Dan confided that he had a problem with his grandson, who disliked him. The ten year old questioned Dan's relationships and attacked his lifestyle. He wanted to know what his grandmother had done wrong. When Dan tried to brush him aside with a curt, "It's none of your business," the bond between them, if it ever existed, came to an abrupt end. "From the mouths of babes ye shall hear the truth."

Yet despite all his foibles, Dan is an enigmatic, wonderful guy. He trusts me and is very forthcoming about his personal relationships, his businesses and the world around him.

That's why Dan is not his real name.

MASTER SMITH ET AL

I was well known as a buyer of second-hand silver and jewelry. I paid immediately. My checks were good. I paid prices that were fair and kept my promise of discretion. I also followed the letter and spirit of the law.

For example, when two teenagers came to sell Georgian English Sterling flatware – 108 pieces in all – and wanted $600 for this exquisite Kings pattern set, I thought it was not kosher so I declined their kind offer. Imagine my surprise when one of them responded and said if their initial price was too high, perhaps I would consider $400!

The law requires buyers, like myself, to be licensed and fingerprinted. Every purchase must be documented in detail and a copy of the transaction must be sent to the Police. The goods bought must be held intact for eighteen days for checking and clearance.

The 30 year old woman had a pretty 1920's platinum ring with an old-European cut center diamond surrounded by small diamonds in an attractive symmetrical design, enhanced by delicate filigree work and hand-engraving. It was a desirable object and I was pleased to pay $3,500 for the ring. She was thrilled to obtain that price. A win-win situation. Or so I thought. Imagine my shock, when the police called to say they thought the ring was "stolen property" and I was not to sell it, pending further investigation. An elderly woman hobbled into my office accompanied by a police officer the next day and indeed identified the ring as hers. It turned out that the vendor was her own daughter, who had stolen it from her and sold it to me. I was obliged to return the ring to its rightful owner. I had no chance of recovery for my loss, as the daughter was an addict, who had no assets to attach. She spent my money on drugs.

Generally people who wanted to sell to me made appointments. Not so, shall we call him, Master Smith.

He just "pitched up," dragging his footlocker of great silver. Smith was an athletic man in his thirties, very articulate and quite charming.

We haggled quite a bit late in the afternoon before we agreed on a price of $2,000 for the assortment of hollowware and flatware, all inherited from his grandmother. Then there was a hitch. We had tendered our check but Smith wanted cash. How could he be sure our check was good, he asked. We tried to reassure him by pointing out the millions of dollars in inventory, the prestigious certificates on our walls and the fact we had been in business at the same address for 15 years. And he could cash our check at our bank the very next morning.

Smith made such a fuss about preferring payment in bills that even after he left with our check, I felt suspicious. I called my contact at Montgomery Police Secondhand Division, and Maureen who headed that division, went into her computer and found our Mr. Smith was an escaped convict.

They arrested him at 9 a.m. the following day as the bank opened. My check had been stopped, so he would not have been paid.

Six months later, I had to deliver testimony in the court at Upper Marlboro, Maryland. I identified the vendor and listened to the facts of the case. A social worker, affiliated with the prison where Smith had been held, testified he was a model prisoner who warranted special training to succeed in the outside world after serving his time. She agreed to his instruction in locksmithing. When this was announced, the formal proceedings in court disintegrated into disbelief and laughter. Order was restored. Needless to say, Smith was a good student and used his newly acquired skills to escape from prison. That very week, while an elderly couple who owned an antique store in Southern Virginia were asleep upstairs above the shop, Smith broke into and entered their establishment and loaded up their pickup truck with their inventory of silver and other goodies.

When the victimized antique dealers heard I had followed my concerns and called the police, they were so grateful to have recovered their uninsured assets, they offered me a reward which I declined. I had not earned it. I was just looking out for myself.

I believe that Master Smith, the master locksmith, is still in prison today.

RED IS GREEN

I was on the sales floor when the distinguished couple walked in and asked if I was the owner.

They introduced themselves as Mr. and Mrs. Winton "Red" Blount, Jr. from Montgomery, Alabama, and had seen our advertisement in the *Washington Post*. They thought we might have what they wanted, a few items for Mrs. Blount (who had forgotten to include her jewelry box) to wear to a White House dinner that evening.

The name Blount meant nothing to me. The fact he was President Richard Nixon's appointee in 1969 to the prestigious office of Postmaster General, then a member of the Cabinet, was unknown to me. So was his being one of the world's largest players in the construction business. He had also served as President of the U.S. Chamber of Commerce.

I learned later that in 1972, Winton Blount ran as a Republican candidate for the U.S. Senate, having none other than George Walker Bush as a campaign assistant. Blount lost to incumbent John Sparkman.

Carolyn Blount was tall and beautiful and moved with much grace. She was reserved and looked to her husband to make the decisions. He had excellent taste and was very decisive. They were very much in love.

The selections came to $95,000, a very substantial sum to us at the time. Payment was tendered in the form of a check with an offer to check him out. Which I did. "Give him the store," said my bank manager.

Madison Avenue experts will tell you that 50 percent of your advertising expenditure is useless. Also, no one knows in advance which 50 percent. Here our tiniest institutional advertisement in the local newspaper, perhaps costing $200 brought in an instant sale of almost 100 grand!

After our transaction was complete, we chatted. Red told me his business took off after he and his brother bought World War II surplus earth-moving equipment from the U.S. Army.

Then he added, he also had a factory making grain-cleaning equipment. I could hardly believe it when he added the name "Clipper"; for that was the brand I bought in my plant. His equipment was being used in Worcester, South Africa. I showed him the annual report of my public company with pictures of our newest feed mill, the product range of our cereals and vegetable oils. With this agribusiness connection in common, we became close friends. This wonderful relationship between the Blounts and us was to last for many years.

Red told me Shakespeare's work was very important to him, so much so he had endowed The Carolyn Blount Theatre in Montgomery, Alabama at a cost of $21,500,000. It enjoys the distinction of being "the finest Shakespearian theatre in the world." Over a million school kids have attended productions at the Montgomery Theatre. He was also a supporter of the Folger Shakespeare Library in Washington, D.C.

When Red endowed a new museum of fine arts in his home town some years later, Zelda and I were invited to be his guests for a long weekend. Speak of southern hospitality! We had a car and driver at our disposal for every hour we were in Montgomery.

The original art at his corporate headquarters was impressive. We were invited to a series of formal dinners, parties and casual brunches. Despite his numerous other guests, he made us feel welcome and special. Royalty could not have been treated with more attention.

J. Carter Brown, the Director of the National Gallery of Art, was the other Washington guest, and the weekend gave us the opportunity to get to know this remarkable man.

Red Blount built a lake near the Arts Museum. He told us how, on a visit to Scotland, he had seen a flock of swans complement the beauty of the water near his hotel. He was determined to do the same for his lake back home. He called the hotel manager and made enquiries as to the source of the swans. Lo and behold, he was told that they had acquired their swans from a farmer thirty miles out of Montgomery, Alabama, U.S.A.!

We were privileged to supply to the Blount Corporation with silver presentation pieces on the occasion of the opening of the $2 billion King Saud University in Riyadh, Saudi Arabia, which Blount, Inc. built. A festive dinner took place to mark the occasion, and Red was placed next to a Prince whose wristwatch Red admired. The prince removed the watch and gave it to Red, who was very embarrassed. I saw the watch, a limited edition Patek Philippe studded with diamonds. Big bucks!

Shirley, Red's vice president and personal assistant, sent us a few dozen of his personal cards so that we could write a personal message to accompany each of the numerous gifts we shipped on his behalf over the years.

I remember Red calling me and saying, "Izzy, I have this wedding in Philadelphia. Good friends. Irish. Do you have anything Irish?" I did not hesitate for a moment. The magnificent Georgian Irish coffee pot was polished, wrapped first in multiple layers of blood red tissue paper, plain newsprint, and then boxed and double-boxed with the appropriate good wishes card from the Blounts. It was sent the very same day.

Red Blount passed away in 2002 at the age of eighty-one. Upon learning of his death, President George W. Bush said Mr. Blount had been "an outstanding leader" and praised "his public service to his community, state and nation." Mr. Blount was active in civic, cultural and charitable work. In his lifetime, he gave away tens of millions of dollars to charities.

We shall always remember him as a big thinker, a man of great vision with the guts to follow through. He was a charming gentleman who left our world a far better place.

Izzy Heller

RED AND CAROLYN BLOUNT

Secrets of a Jeweler

THE CAROLYN BLOUNT THEATRE

FAIR COMPENSATION?

Over my three-score-and-ten years on this planet, I should have learned to take note of warning signals. In the case of Eric Grunwald, my employee, I did not.

Eric applied to us for a job towards the end of 1998, just before our busy Christmas season. We were short-staffed and we needed a sales associate to cope with the inevitable rush, so we employed him.

His experience in retail was O.K. He had worked for three years at a small independent and then for one year at a large jewelry guild store.

But Eric marginally passed the Reid Psychological questionnaire. The results indicated he was a borderline candidate in terms of integrity.

The other warning signal was he had been fired from his previous position, having traded in jewelry privately on the side.

Two little bells rang in my head, but the expediency of the moment silenced both of them and he started work at the beginning of October.

Eric was a pleasant addition to our staff and in a short while became reasonably knowledgeable about our product mix. He worked well with clients and I hoped we had made a good appointment, although there were little incidents that unsettled me. I overlooked them.

At that time, we decided to flood Chevy Chase with direct mail solicitations. Our computer produced gummed labels with our clients' names and addresses and we had the tedious task of attaching them to 20,000 leaflets. There was some urgency because we had to effect home delivery before Thanksgiving.

Eric Grunwald had five children and he offered to take some mailings and labels home one night to expedite the job. I offered to compensate the kids for their efforts. So Eric took the store handcart, placed two boxes of leaflets on it and wheeled it to his car. The next morning he returned with the labels duly affixed. We were thrilled to have the help.

Secrets of a Jeweler

We were not so pleased to hear a week later Eric hurt his back in lifting the twenty pound boxes of leaflets. Nor were we pleased, quite separately, to receive a Court Order to withhold income for child support.

We immediately reported his back pain to the Workers' Compensation Commission as required by law. Eric resigned and left our employ three months after he started. He has not worked since.

As I write this, almost six years later, the Hartford Insurance Company has paid out over $300,000.00 for this claim and it is an ongoing commitment for the insurer as long as Eric is temporarily or totally disabled. All legal appeals have failed.

The payments include items like:

- wages
- medical costs
- hospitalization
- disability
- emergency care
- surgery costs
- aquatic therapy
- physical therapy
- psychiatric referral
- instruction in the use of a TENS unit

The Workers' Compensation Fund draws from contributions of employers and employees. If claims are high, premiums go up.

In the case of Eric Grunwald, one wonders: did he receive FAIR COMPENSATION?

MY GENERAL MANAGER

The following is the eulogy I delivered for my General Manager, Solly Dektor, who happened to be my wife's father.

"SOLOMON A. DEKTOR . . .

S. A. D. . . .

This is a SAD day in the chronicles of the Dektor family which includes in America now the Hellers and the Messecas.

How we have grown since Alma and Joe Gildenhorn sponsored Zelda and me to this country some thirteen years ago.

Solly and Fay Dektor followed their children to these shores and immigrated from South Africa three years ago. This was the second emigration for Solly.

As a family of recent immigrants, we have had our lot cast into American society. We have paid our initiation dues and our taxes. However the inevitable certainties of life includes not only taxes, but alas, also death.

Since Zelda and I arrived in the States, we have enjoyed family birthdays, anniversaries, weddings, births, and indeed more immigrations. We knew that sooner or later we would have to face up to a funeral. That forearmed knowledge does not make this day any easier to bear. It is a sad day.

But this day brings with it the opportunity to relate a beautiful LOVE STORY.

Solly Dektor was born in the little town of Rokiskis, Lithuania – one of seven children who were to be dispersed in time among Russia, Israel, South Africa and America. Solly was instructed at the Yeshiva College in Kovno and the Yeshiva Bocher became very conversant with Jewish teachings. Over the years, Solly would illustrate a point in dialogue by quoting in Hebrew from the scriptures. He was multilingual – speaking

Hebrew, Yiddish, Russian, Afrikaans and English – five languages in all. The fact that he was afflicted with a stammer did not preclude him from communicating effectively.

Solly's father, like his son-in-law to be, was in the grain trade and had a flour mill. But Solly did not join his Dad in business for it was decided to save him from the Russian army by sending him off to South Africa. Before he left he was trained for a career in jewelry. In his late teens, a penniless foreigner who could speak no English, he got off the boat in Cape Town Harbor.

Now enters the second character to this love story, a South African born girl, one FAY LEVY, a pretty sixteen year old secretary in a large household appliance organization.

Her parents had arranged some three years earlier that she should marry a certain CARL, the third character to complete this love triangle. Carl was some nine hundred miles to the north, near Johannesburg. But what was distance, when the bridegroom owned land on top of one of the richest gold reefs in the world? Fay Levy was "bespoken for," as the saying went, by Carl.

The Levy parents were not at all pleased with the new suitor, Solly – this up-start alien who had nothing.

That did not stop Solly. He and Fay were secretly engaged and for several years had to hide their modest engagement ring while waiting until Solly's elder sister could find a husband.

When Fay was all of twenty in the year 1935, she married Solly. They were so excited. They had saved for a one-day honeymoon, six miles down the road at a local hotel. When they returned, Solly's little jewelry store had been burgled and they started life together from ground zero.

Who said the words "parents always know better"? Solly and Fay set off on a fifty seven-year partnership of love that knew no equal. Their alliance was made in heaven. Mutual trust, selfless devotion and endless affection were the pillars of their relationship. They were good Jewish homemakers and enthusiastic Zionists, the salt of the community in which they lived. Their home was open to all and the lonely knew they could visit at any time. There is a round synagogue near the slopes of Table Mountain

– Solly and Fay were observant members of that congregation since its inception. They were ever proud of their family in particular of their two children Zelda and Leslie.

Solly's drive and charm assured him of a successful business career. His friend and close partner was Bill Peters. The partners could not have been more different. The 6'3" Wasp weighed three hundred pounds. The 5'5" Jew weighed half that. The administrator and the marketer. The accelerator pedal and the brake pedal. What a team! They could not fail. Phoenix Electrical of Long Street, Cape Town flourished and grew to be one of the most successful endeavors of its kind. Sol was so proud when he began to serve the third generation of customers, all of whom were his friends. Amongst the Indian community he became fondly know as "Doctor Dapter."

In a society that regarded Racism as a norm, these two men stood out. For they would not be party to any facet of APARTHEID. Solly was active in liberal politics and was a close colleague of Harry Lawrence, the Minister of Justice in General Smuts' war time cabinet who did a lot for refugees from Europe. Bill Peters went on to become Mayor of Cape Town. In fact, he was in office and hosted the Mayor of Washington, DC, Mr. Walter Washington, when he visited South Africa.

When World War II commenced, Solly was one of the first volunteers to go up North. Even when he was rejected for health reasons, he proudly served in the Home Guard.

Solly's store had a big advertising sign on the front of its building. It also had an invisible marker on the street pavement. A marker which could be read by the homeless and less fortunate which said "there's a soft touch inside." Solly could never refuse a hand outstretched in need. In a tribute to his social contributions, he was given many ovations when he left South Africa, including one from the homeless of Long Street. Both Solly and Fay were active contributors to charities of all kind.

Only a few days ago in the kingdom of his Chevy Chase bedroom, this frail figure – cum fractures and all – would smile, try to raise his brittle bones and do his personal rendition of the Home Guard March – all to cheer us up.

Secrets of a Jeweler

Considering that Solly had been stricken by ill health many times, we are grateful to have had him with us for his 84th birthday. Thirty-five years ago he was laid low by a serious heart attack. An aneurysm in the chest struck him down five years back. And last year, pneumonia.

Solly was a man of his word. Often to his detriment, his word was his bond. So in 1992 - to fulfill a promise to his baby brother to be with him for his 80th birthday, he took off for Israel and encountered its worst winter. He came back only to be rushed to the hospital. He was not one to complain, even when terminal cancer reared its ugly head three months ago. Many times he told me he was grateful, for life had been good to him.

In the Oncology Department at Sibley Hospital – like anywhere else he went – everyone was his friend. His self-appointed role was to cheer up his fellow patients. In sixty seconds a stranger would become a buddy. He was so endearing. He was a hugger and kisser and he would distribute his "old world charm" generously and indiscriminately.

But all of us have failings. Solly too. He was a SHOWOFF, a peacock. This dapper romantic was always beautifully groomed with every gray hair on his head – and above his lips – in place. His fob chain, which Leslie proudly received last night, and his tie pin, which I gratefully wear today, were part of his basic wardrobe. Some days he would sport a rose on his lapel. Only a few hours before his passing away, he insisted on having his facial cologne. He was a dignified, elegant man to the end.

I first met Solly thirty six years ago when I started courting his daughter. I can truthfully say that in that entire period of time there has never been the hint of an argument between us. And even if there had been a dispute or a difference with me or anyone else, it could not fester. No grudge could be held by Solly. For in his own words, he had a special place next to his heart. His own private little cemetery between his ribs. If ever there developed the hint of a grudge, he would take it, compress it and bury it immediately in his private cemetery.

Such was his zest for life that when he arrived in America, he decided to return to his original profession – that of jeweler. Soon he was pouring over books in my library reminding himself – so he said – that an aquamarine and an emerald were first cousins of beryl. And that a VVS2 was better than a SI1 diamond.

He was never invited to join the team. He knew he did not have to be. He just took keys to the showcases and started serving at Heller Jewelers. The customers loved him. And he sold brilliantly. Just as in the good old days. He didn't want and didn't get a salary check. His reward was the business card that read Solomon A. Dektor, General Manager. And if he could rush to open the door for a young lady, that was his bonus. It was a privilege for me to work with him.

Earlier I spoke of a love story. I must also refer to the tragedy of the last three months.

This tragedy had its hero, Solly, who was a brave patient. But it also had three heroines, a wife, a daughter and a granddaughter. Fay, Zelda and Tania. I salute these three magnificent angels, who ensured that for every second of the long twenty four hours which made up each day and night for the last three months, there was a huge cushion of total love to comfort Solly, to ease his pain and to show sincere affection. Anything that could be done – no matter what – was done by these three women. Solly was well aware of their committed devotion to him.

Even in his time of supreme crisis, Solly was happy. Proud of his daughter's recent award in the real estate field. And when the phone rang three weeks ago, on the very day of his 84th birthday, to tell him that his son had been awarded, by the Directors Guild of America, their top honor "Director of the Year" – he felt that his cup was running over with *NACHAS*.

Our scriptures tell us that between last Rosh Hashanah and Yom Kippur, that is in the period between September 28, 1992 and October 7, 1992 – awesome decisions were made. Then it was determined who would live and who would die. And one of those decisions taken was that "the light and life" of Solomon Alec Dektor would be taken from him, and from us, peacefully in the early morning hours of Friday 26 March 1993.

Is there any legacy to his life on earth? I think so. In fact several. I'll name just four of the treasures:

Daniel Saul Messeca of Bethesda

Ariel Joseph Messeca of Bethesda

Gabriella Tamar Harris Heller of Chicago

Benjamin Solomon Harris Heller of Chicago

Please allow me to make a prediction. In the year 2010 – 17 years from now – when millions of people applaud the crowning of Miss America, a young lady from Chicago, they will look at their TV sets and see the big round eyes of Solly Dektor.

So we say farewell to my beloved father-in-law, my beloved friend – to all the world a character, a gentleman and a *mensch*!

Izzy Heller

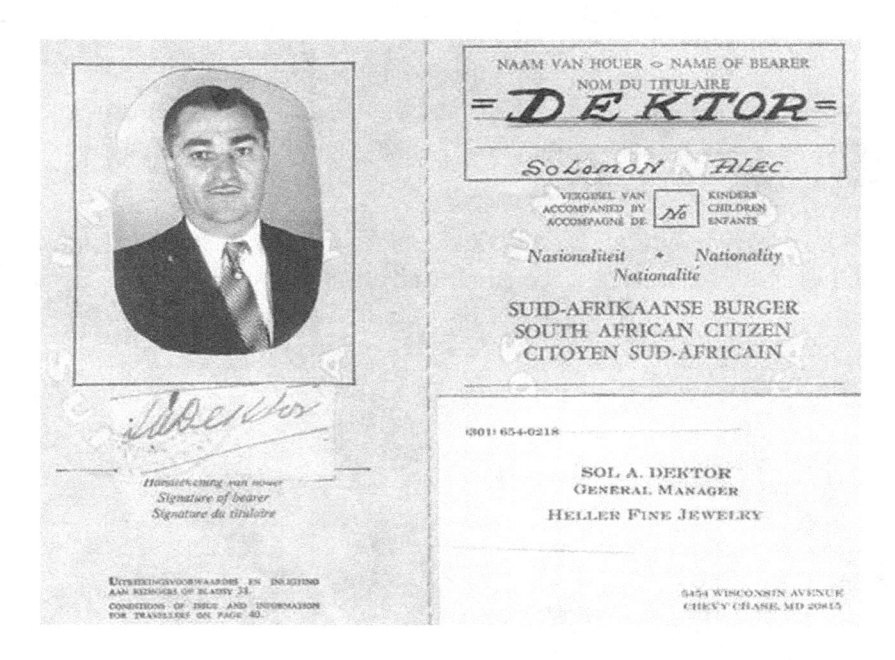

SOUTH AFRICAN PASSPORT OF S.A. DEKTOR WITH LATER BUSINESS CARD

THE TIFFANY NAME

In 1992, a man from Gaithersburg visited my store and said he had 20 items of Tiffany glass to sell. He remembered we had a large display of Art Glass in our store some while earlier and consequently thought we might like to buy and stock his collection.

Zelda and I have always loved the design, the colors and joy of Tiffany glass – mainly the lamps and vases. So did the market and that's why they were pricey.

We visited Mr. George's home in Gaithersburg that day after we closed the store. It was a modest house with a sparsely illuminated interior. In the dim light, the 20 pieces glowed.

Mr. George said his grandfather had been a keen collector of Tiffany glassware and he wanted to hold back one item for the family. He would sell the remainder for $10,000. We settled for $9,500, made out a bill of sale and paid him then and there. We carefully packed and loaded our car with the vases, lamps and ink bottles and returned to our home on Charred Oak Drive in Bethesda.

What a difference bright light makes. The glass was "nice from far" but up close, it was "far from nice." There were just things that disturbed me. The weight, the signature, etc.

My investigation confirmed my suspicion and I wrote to Mr. George asking for a refund. The response was a letter from his attorney which reads as follows:

Dear Mr. Heller:

    I am writing to you in response to your letter to Mr. George dated September 25, 1992.

    It is my understanding that my client contacted your company to inquire as to the authenticity and resale value of a collection of glass which he purchased at Virginia Beach. He indicates that both you and your wife closed your shop and rushed over to his house. After your inspection of the glass and review of the certificate of appraisal, you offered to buy the glass.

Obviously, my client is no expert in these matters and relied on the experience and expertise of you and Mrs. Heller. My client has no independent knowledge of the authenticity of this glass. He relied on your opinion and that of your wife, as well as the appraisal.

My client made no representation regarding the authenticity of the glass and he has no independent knowledge as to whether this glass is Tiffany Glass or otherwise.

I strongly suggest that you investigate the matter to determine the facts before you file suit.

My client does not intend to make any refund based on the information which you have provided to him. If you have any questions, please ask your lawyer to contact me.

Sincerely,

I was furious when I saw how the truth had been twisted. Mr. George had signed the bill of sale stating "warranted Tiffany." I decided that a civil suit was not enough to nail Mr. George.

I filed criminal charges in the District Court of Maryland and my sworn statement read as follows:

I, the undersigned, apply for a statement of charges and a summons or warrant which may lead to the arrest of the above-named Defendant because on or about September 3, 1992 in Gaithersburg, Maryland, the above-named Defendant knowingly deceived me and my wife into paying him the sum of $9.500.00 for 19 items of glassware which he verbally and in writing warranted as being made by the famous house of "TIFFANY" in the early part of this century, when he was well aware that this was not so. When my wife and I returned home with the glass items purchased, we examined them under better light and became suspicious. [Mr. George had

Secrets of a Jeweler

guaranteed the origin of the 20-piece collection as being inherited from his late grandfather, who "had collected them in the early 1900's." He kept one piece "for sentimental reasons because he was attached to his grandfather," he said. He sold us the 19 other items of glass.] Shortly thereafter, we photographed our purchase. The two top auction houses in the world are Sotheby's and Christies. Their New York experts stated they were not Tiffany made. A local expert, Bill Weschler, who examined some of the glass said they are "fake." When confronted, Mr. George admitted the glass was not inherited. He stated they were made in the 1940's. (Tiffany stopped manufacture of glass in 1928.) The glass is still in our possession. We have offered it back to Mr. George and asked for a refund, which he refuses.

I solemnly affirm under the penalties of perjury that the contents of this Application are true to the best of my knowledge, information and belief.

Israel Heller

The Montgomery County, Maryland police responded quickly and served notice to Mr. George, who refunded our money even quicker, took back his glass and apologized profusely for "the misunderstanding." Obviously, he didn't want a jail sentence for his fraud. We dropped the charge.

People the world over pay a premium for merchandise bearing the reputable name of Tiffany. Unfortunately, this encourages "knock-offs" like those of Mr. George.

Izzy Heller

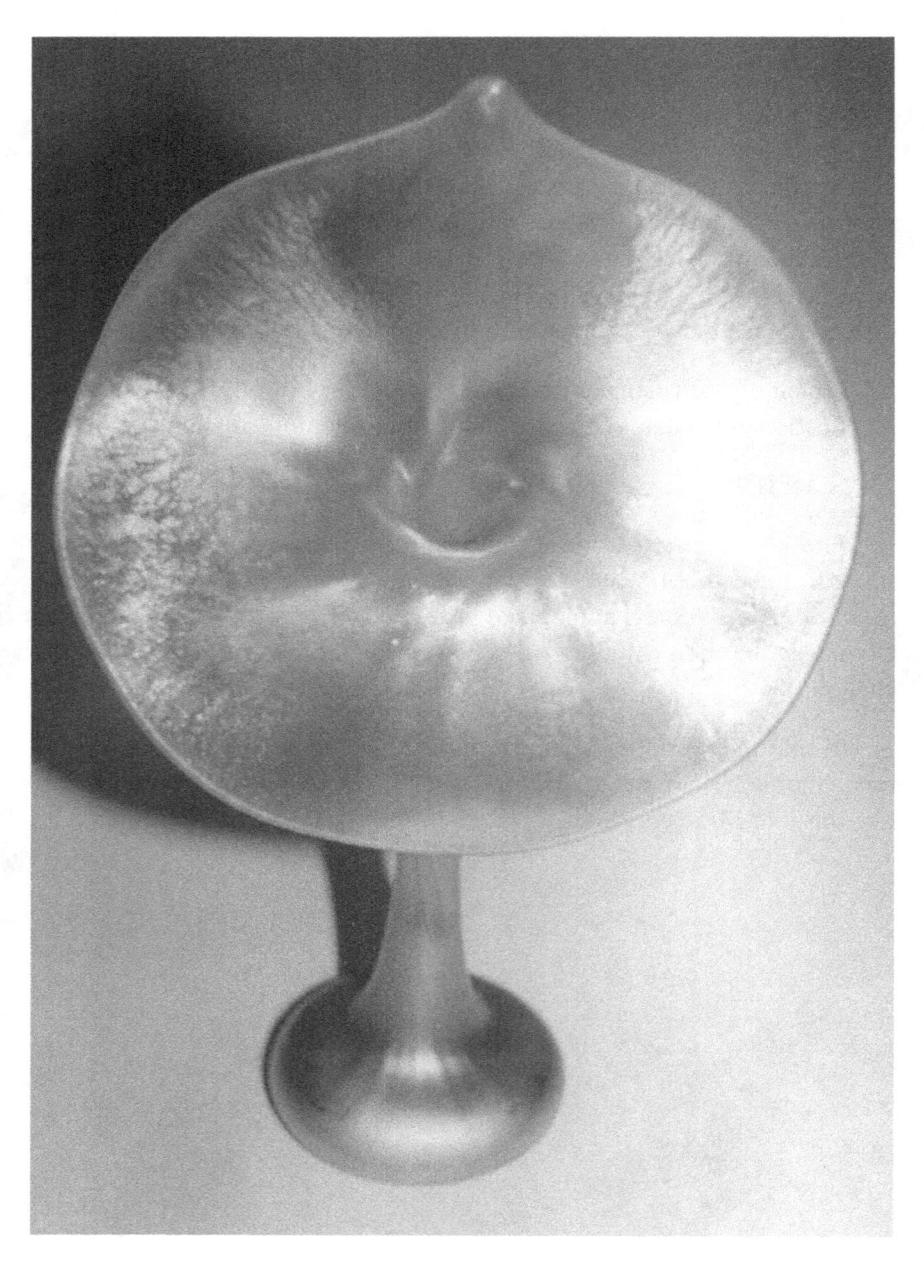

FAUX TIFFANY VASE

Secrets of a Jeweler

FAUX TIFFANY PERFUME BOTTLE

THERE'S NO BUSINESS LIKE SHOW BUSINESS

Based on statistics I have studied, I believe the average retail jeweler in America loses money for six months of the year, breaks-even for three months, and makes a profit for the remaining three months, usually the last of the calendar year.

Contrary to popular belief, that non-existent average man, the average jeweler, makes only 4 percent net profit before income tax on his sales. So on a $1,000 sale, $40 is all his profit, on which he still has to pay federal and state taxes. Certainly this is not a high profit margin considering the security hazards (many jewelers even buy kidnapping insurance) and the high capital requirement.

Profitability can be improved in this capital-intensive business if one can turn over inventory more frequently, say one-and-one-half times, instead of once annually.

To achieve this better utilization of resources tied up in stock, we decided to participate as exhibitors in jewelry shows. Our attempts at New Orleans, Dallas and Philadelphia failed and resulted in losses. We found three cities whose shows were highly profitable: New York, Miami Beach and Las Vegas. Each of these three had it's own distinct character.

One thing all jewelry shows have in common: SECURITY. The show's own, local private security and city police officers are all in attendance, some visible and others in plain clothes. Photo ID's are worn by staff and exhibitors at all times. And yet there are incidents resulting in losses.

The other commonality: SET-UP STAMPEDE. Certain firms pay exhibitor fees primarily to get an initial edge in buying fine one-of-a-kind pieces. So while exhibits are being set up and inventory unpacked, the vultures descend. We would often achieve 80 percent of our show's income the very first day of set-up, before the official opening. When the show opened, we would often see our own pieces in other booths, substantially higher in price.

Deals between dealers often are done on a handshake and the word *MAZAL* (good luck). The buyer takes his purchases with the understanding payment would be made before the show's conclusion. On the show's final day, Zelda would zip around on a scooter picking up checks. Once we had an English dealer disappear on the last day of the show and it took us six months of nagging to get paid. He is the exception to the bond of trust that permeates the industry.

There is an atmosphere of urgency about shows. They are short-lived events. In a few days it's "over-kedover." Decide now or forever hold your peace is the understanding of buyers.

We would have visits from Englishmen, Germans, Italians, Chinese, Swiss and they would kibbitz at our booth about the rate of exchange, our president, their economy and so on. The camaraderie was wonderful. Jokes would be told while we munched nuts, junk food and drank bottled water. It was great fun.

There are considerable costs in "Showing." Apart from staff salaries, travel, hotel and meal expenses, a typical event would involve things like $3,000 for booth rental for a 12' x 8' space, $1,100 for a safe, $300 for a carpet, table and chairs, $1,500 for 3 showcases and $500 for lighting. Zelda liked to have fresh flowers and candy. And in Las Vegas we had a refrigerator – more for the kosher foods of our Chassidic customers, than for our convenience.

New York's Jewelers of America Show is held twice a year, in early February and late July, for four days at a time, in the Jacob Javitz Center, a massive structure on the west side of Manhattan at 12th Avenue and 33rd Street. It is strictly a trade show, and dealers have to be members of Jewelers of America or else listed in the Red Book, a Jewelers Board of Trade credit directory, to be admitted. Ninety five percent of exhibits relate to new jewelry and only five percent for other jewelry, variously referred to as pre-loved, second-hand, estate or antique. I guesstimate the displayed goods in the estate section to be worth about $50 million. So you can imagine the total value in the Center.

The show is vast, over three levels, and cleverly divided into sections or pavilions. Countries like Italy (my favorite) have probably 80 exhibitors. Hong Kong, Thailand, Israel, Spain, Turkey, Great Britain, France,

Germany all have strong representations. There are food stations and restaurants. Lectures are conducted. Suppliers of safes, software, books, display materials and other related products ply their wares. To walk the show, without stopping to chat, takes a day.

The now famous David Yurman has a huge booth at most shows, with perimeter displays on the walls and an interior with several buying offices. His jewelry is stocked by Neiman Marcus, Saks Fifth Avenue and top jewelers in every state of the nation.

When we had just been open a year, we discovered his work and offered to market his products for the Christmas season. We mailed 50,000 illustrated leaflets and placed four ⅛ page adverts in the *Washington Post* to promote the opening on December 12, 1981. David and his wife Sybil, a serious and charming couple, came out to Chevy Chase for the grand opening.

It was not to be. The accumulation of snow on that day was the heaviest in decades and the city of Washington came to a total standstill. It took three days to get access to our store. The no-show cost us many thousands.

Because our strategy was to become more focused on estate and less on new jewelry, we never did another Yurman show. It was our loss.

We "did" the Miami Beach Original Antique Show for 18 years. It accommodates about 1,000 dealers and in addition to our "product mix" of jewelry and silver, there is an abundance of furniture, glass, paintings, carpets, dolls, handbags, books, etc. Held in the last week of January each year, the weather is warm, the attire is casual and (God help us) the public is invited.

This Florida show was an arduous seven-day continuous event starting at 11a.m. and finishing at 10p.m. daily. At the end, we were so exhausted we could hardly pack up to ship via armored car. When Brinks or Dunbar gave us the last signature on the waybills for our footlockers which held millions of dollars of inventory, we were on the verge of collapse from physical exhaustion.

Often we would get on a cruise ship the next day to recover from the taxing ordeal of showtime.

Secrets of a Jeweler

The Miami Beach show was run for many years in a strict fashion by a promoter who was not popular with dealers. He would threaten us over the public address system with the likes of "If you pack up before closing time, you will not be eligible for next year's show." Because of the strong demand for booths, he would get away with his bullying.

Today the show is managed by an international company which has listened to exhibitor complaints and made the show shorter and also made night closings earlier. The atmosphere is much more cordial.

We had a prime location at this show for the eighteen years we exhibited – on a corner, dead center between halls A and B. Initially, we had an African American mama making fudge right across from us. She placed a fan in front of her booth in the belief the fudge aroma was like "the sizzle sells the steak." One hour into the aroma, we swore never to buy fudge again.

Later there was the invasion of the Iranians, who came en masse to occupy a booth next to us. There were probably six dealers who shared the premises. The noise level was deafening and the food supply was something to behold. They were a lively bunch and wonderful neighbors. They were also great traders and we learned a lot from them.

"Privates" or members of the public often regard their visits to this Miami show as an entertainment outing. It certainly was not fun for us to show an expensive diamond necklace to a woman who held a hot dog, dripping with mustard, in one hand and a diet coke in another and who wanted to try it on. Then after looking at herself in our mirror for the umpteenth time, we heard the familiar words, "I'll speak to my husband."

The Miami Beach show occupies a vast area in the Convention Center and Zelda would sometimes rent a scooter to vet the show or make deliveries quickly without wasting time. Once she parked the scooter in front of our booth leaving the keys in the ignition. Our neighboring exhibitor pointed out a woman had taken the little vehicle and was making off with it. I followed in hot pursuit, shouting to security to help. We caught up with the scooter just before the thief was about to ramp it up her pickup truck. She nearly made her getaway. Her explanation: "I was just having some fun." She was taken into custody.

Some years ago, there was a freak rainstorm in southern Florida, which turned the streets around the Miami Beach Convention Center into small rivers. One evening at 10p.m. when we exited the show, we walked eight blocks in water that was ten inches deep. My new sneakers were ruined that night. What an exhilarating ending to a hard day. Life's little challenges come in many forms. With the flood, we departed from our usual routine of dinner on Lincoln or Washington Streets. We could not wait to get back and dry out in our Art Deco hotel, The Richmond on Collins Avenue, owned by our friends the Herberts.

Of course, the largest shows of all were in Las Vegas. In the first week of June, it was held at the Sands Convention Center, virtually 100 percent for new jewelry. We, as estate jewelers, exhibited at the same time in the Rio Hotel from where there was a shuttle bus operating between our show and the Sands.

Las Vegas gets bigger and better each year. Its big jewelry shows do not admit members of the public. The hours are normally from 10a.m. to 6p.m. and the atmosphere is relaxed and playful. Gaming, what a nice word for gambling, and spectacular nightly performances are a few yards away and put everyone in a holiday spirit. Here in Vegas, we picked up new clients from the west coast, mainly Los Angeles and San Francisco, just short shuttle flights away.

Of all the shows where we exhibited, Zelda and I will miss Las Vegas most, she for the gaming, me for the desert which I love.

We also went to two great cities for the express purpose of buying. These were Tucson, Arizona for gems and Basel, Switzerland for jewelry.

The Smithsonian Institution's annual lecture series on gemstones to "rockhounds" was a prime factor in the initiation of Tucson as a world center for trading precious stones. The first week of February would become the time to "Mecca-out" in Arizona. Today there are many different shows each with hundreds of exhibitors. Thousands of buyers converge on the city and accommodations, rental cars and restaurant reservations are at their limits of availability.

At the time of my first visit, Tucson gem shows were in their infancy. They were scattered across the city in dozens of hotels, halls and open-air locations.

I'll always remember the Holiday Inn, where I walked down the center passage on an upper floor. The doors to the bedrooms were all open, each housing an exhibitor who would show his wares by day on the very bed on which he would rest at night.

One such room housed a Colombian couple with a baby. The child was good. The emeralds were better. I like to think I knew what I was doing when I spent $30,000 with them. Did I secure beautiful stones from the famed Muzor mines! Vivid greens with only small inclusions.

And so it went, from room to room. My briefcase bulged from my purchases of sapphires, rubies, amethysts, tourmalines and kunzites. I went to the post office twice daily to send boxes by registered mail back home.

I did extremely well with those gemstones. We designed rings, pins and necklaces to accommodate them and most sold very quickly.

Visitors to Tucson at that time of year enjoy crisp desert air and the smell of citrus trees. It reminded me of the town of Montagu about one hundred miles from Cape Town.

Now to Europe. The geography of Basel is interesting. The boundaries of three countries meet there. The airport is on French soil, our hotel was in Germany and the show was in Switzerland. All within a few miles of one another.

The Hotel Romerbad in Badenweiler, Germany, is one of the finest hotels in the world. It is located alongside volcanic hot springs, which the Romans made famous.

When Zelda and I visited Basel in April of 1984, the hotel provided a luxury bus for the show attendees, which left at 9:30a.m. each morning and picked us up at 5:30p.m. for the return trip, crossing an international border on each occasion.

In the evenings we took a swim in the hotel's wonderful pool and then would either enjoy the formality of their main dining room or venture out to the little town for dinner.

It was the season for asparagus. White "spargel" had its own menu and was served in thirty different ways, each delicious. The over-sized spears are soft from stem to tip and the German chefs got us coming back again and again.

The town of Badenweiler is near the Black Forest and is famous not only for its hot baths but also for its cuckoo clocks. In one shop, there were thousands of these crazy clocks. I previously thought they were cute, but after seeing a National Geographic TV program, where the cuckoo steals the eggs of other birds and raises the chicks as her own, I became very "anti-cuckoo."

It's easy to part with money on nice things at the Basel Show and we did just that. In two days we spent some $400,000, half of which went to the Chen Brothers.

At that time, merchandise from Hong Kong was inexpensive and the house of Chen was the best of the island's exhibitors. David Chen received us warmly and introduced us to his range. Beautifully designed, well executed and affordably priced, his jewelry seduced us. We were a little apprehensive to blow 50 percent of our budget on one supplier, but our brave decision proved to be correct for we sold virtually all Chen's items before the year was out.

David Chen visited us in Washington the next year. We invited him home for dinner. As was his custom, he removed his shoes at the front door. We had a great evening and learned of his addiction to the racing of dogs and horses.

Success in the jewelry industry requires the clever working of shows, whether for buying or selling. We certainly did well with them and believe for the profit and the excitement, there is no business like show business.

Secrets of a Jeweler

HOTEL ROMERBAD, BADENWEILER

DIVORCE, SOUTH AFRICAN STYLE

Because we at Heller Jewelers had secure premises with a walk-in bank vault, friends would leave valuables with us for safekeeping.

Insurance companies only cover jewelry in transit while in the possession of the named insured or when in a vault with a jeweler like ourselves. Our facilities were therefore used by many traveling salesmen for overnight safekeeping so they could relax at dinner or a movie without lugging around a bag of heavy jewelry.

A visiting couple from South Africa who were close friends and who got their green cards to immigrate here asked us to store some of their valuables for several months while they went back to Johannesburg in preparation for the final move to the U.S. with their family.

They left with us a gold coin collection including 50 Kruger Rands, antique jewelry, diamond rings, imperial jade carvings, pearl necklaces and the like. It was enough to serve as the starting inventory of a kiosk operation in a jewelry mall. We placed their treasures in sealed boxes in a locked safe within our vault.

The process of emigration causes severe psychological strain, as we knew only too well. The prospect of separation from family and friends is stressful. Even before one's arrival in a new homeland, one's emotional well-being will have been tested.

That was the case with Walter and Sandra, the owners of the collection in our vault. There may have been prior problems, but now they had the okay to come to the States, they had to face up to the reality that both of them would have to work to survive (she did not in Joh'burg) and they would have to face a severe drop in their standard of living.

One day, we received a phone call advising of a delay in their arrival date and in a subsequent conversation Sandra confided to Zelda her relationship with Walter was deteriorating.

Months later they decided to separate and when I heard the news, I knew what was coming.

Sure enough, there came a very formal fax from Walter stating they were getting a divorce and he alone was the owner of the valuables. He would instruct me in due course as to the disposition. I did not reply.

Weeks later Sandra called Zelda and told her the news of the breakup in their marriage and Walter had moved out. She very casually "reminded" Zelda "the goodies" were hers. Zelda did not comment.

Zelda and I discussed the matter at length and came up with a solution worthy of King Solomon.

We wrote each spouse the same letter:

> Dear Walter/Sandra:
>
> Your items entrusted to us are safe here in our vault at 5454 Wisconsin Avenue, Chevy Chase, Maryland.
>
> They will remain here until we receive written advice to the contrary, such advice to be agreed upon and signed by BOTH OF YOU.
>
> We are your dear friends.

Love,
Zelda and Izzy

It took a long time for them to agree, but agree they did.

In their settlement arrangement, Sandra got the sealed boxes, which she took back to South Africa.

Neither Walter nor Sandra has settled in the States. Walter has remarried and has a child with his new wife. He says he is quite happy. Sandra is on her own and says she is very unhappy. They see each other occasionally at functions held by one of their four children. Such is divorce, South African style.

HIS OWN WORST ENEMY

"Diamonds are forever"

"Diamonds are a girl's best friend"

"I never hated a man enough to give him his diamonds back"

These quotations confirm what we all know, namely diamonds are the most valuable treasures known to mankind. They are also the hardest substance known.

For some unknown reason, no natural diamond has crystallized in the last ten million years.

Every diamond in the world is unique. No two are the same.

The color in a natural colored diamond is a result of an impurity in the otherwise pure carbon.

Over 300,000 Indian workers are employed in the diamond industry in Bombay. Other important distribution centers like Antwerp, New York, Tel Aviv and Johannesburg also provide large employment, not to mention production areas like Australia, Southern Africa, Canada and Russia.

I can go on and on reciting interesting facts about these little stones.

One certainty is that DIAMONDS ATTRACT CROOKS.

Moshe Benjamin was a diamond dealer based in Toronto, Canada who had access to and traded on the floors of the New York and Antwerp diamond bourses.

He gained the confidence of his peers in Belgium to the extent he could outwit them to the tune of some $15 million worth of diamonds. Apparently, he gained access to a communal vault and brazenly stole from the inventory of several traders.

Immediately the news of the theft went on the wire and all diamond exchanges were alerted. Publication was in the trade press and we in the

Secrets of a Jeweler

New York Diamond Dealers Club saw Moshe's photo under an FBI wanted notice.

Despite all the publicity, Moshe was nowhere to be found.

Several years later, on a brisk fall morning, a tourist bus was about to leave Toronto for Niagara Falls, which involved crossing the Canadian/U.S. border.

As is often the habit, a U.S. customs officer boarded the stationary bus, walked down the aisle and asked whether there was "anything to declare." Negative was the unanimous response.

The officer was about to alight when she looked back and saw one passenger clutching his briefcase rather protectively. He looked down when she made eye contact with him. She approached him and asked him to open his case, which was filled with documents. The very top paper caught the customs official's attention because it had the picture of the passenger on it. Indeed it was the FBI notice, wanting Moshe Benjamin. He was promptly arrested.

He was his own worst enemy.

THE TOKYO CONNECTION

Most people who have studied diamonds will have heard of the Cullinan. It was a stone found in South Africa weighing 3,106 carats. When first seen in the mine, the superintendent thought he was being fooled by a large piece of glass, but tests proved it to be the largest gem-quality diamond ever discovered.

Allow me to quote from the G.I.A. Diamond Dictionary. "The stone was sold to the Transvaal Government, which presented it to King Edward VII on his 66th birthday, November 9, 1907. It was insured for $1,250,000 when it was sent to England. The King entrusted the cutting of the Cullinan to the famous Asscher's Diamond Co. in Amsterdam, which had cut the Excelsior and other large gems. The huge diamond was studied for months. On February 10, 1908, Mr. Asscher placed a steel cleaver's blade in a previously prepared V-shaped groove and tapped it once with a heavy steel rod; the blade broke but the diamond remained intact! On the second attempt however, it fell apart exactly as planned. A second cleavage in the same direction produced three principal sections; these, in turn, were divided into nine major gems, ninety-six smaller brilliants and nine and one-half carats of unpolished pieces. The nine large stones remain either in the British Crown Jewels or in the personal possession of the Royal Family. This historically celebrated gem and it's present mounting is as follows: *Cullinan I,* the largest fashioned diamond in the world, is called the *Great Star of Africa.* It is a 75-facet pear-shaped stone and weighs 530.20 carats. Kind Edward placed it in the Sovereign's Royal Scepter as part of the Crown Jewels, and it is now on display in the Tower of London."

All this is by way of letting the reader know that Joseph Asscher was a genius in the diamond trade and his family's patented make or cut of a highly brilliant form of square step cut diamond remained in demand since 1910 when it was developed and has been copied into the 21st Century. The Asscher-cut diamond has recently been described as "the hottest rock in Hollywood."

The distinguishing characteristics of the diamonds which bore his name include long parallel facets, called steps, both on the crown (top) and

Secrets of a Jeweler

pavilion (bottom) of the stone, as well as a small table with a steep crown and cut corners, giving the stone not only great reflection of light and much brilliance of color, but also an old-world charm.

Extremely scarce, an Asscher sells as soon as it is put in a showcase. So jewelers like myself considered themselves fortunate to have an Asscher diamond in its original custom-made ring mounting. I had such a ring.

I was surprised to receive the enquiry, and even more so, from a New York lady with an Oriental accent. How did she come to us? She replied stating the Estate Jewelers Association of America had referred her to us. Yes, I said, we do have a 1920's Asscher diamond ring.

She took down the details of the five carat stone and within an hour phoned again to say she would buy the ring at the $65,000 quoted. I thanked her for the order and asked when she would come to see the ring and finalize the transaction. No, she stated, that would not be possible as she had a baby only a few weeks old, but she would give us an American Express card number to charge the sale which she agreed would be final. She also referred us to her husband, a partner in a law firm.

I was pleased to have such a large sale but could not comfortably sell on a basis of "sight unseen." Also, at the time, we were only a few weeks away from our busy Christmas season and knowing the ring would sell out of our showroom, I did not feel like shipping it, only to get is back a month later.

We negotiated an arrangement whereby Zelda would take the U.S. Airways shuttle to New York, meet the customer at La Guardia airport, show her the ring and see if she still wished to purchase it. If so, the payment would be effected and Zelda would immediately take the next shuttle home.

It was a snowy day and flights were delayed when Zelda flew to New York that December day. But she did it. A pretty, delicate Japanese lady met her at the terminal. With no seats in the arrival section, they sat together on the concrete floor in a corner where she admired the ring, saw the G.I.A. certificate and confirmed the purchase. She signed the invoice and the American Express voucher both endorsed with the phrase "final sale – no return, no refund, no exchange."

The following day, our client's husband called to say how happy we had made his wife and how he appreciated the effort we had made to ensure their satisfaction.

That was that, we thought. Another successful sale.

But it was not to be. Two months later, the New York lawyer was on the phone to me, asking whether we would take the ring back.

He was very apologetic. He was prepared to take a big loss. But his wife could no longer wear the ring because it turned out to be tragically unlucky.

It appears that his wife had been admiring the diamond that morning as she had every day since she acquired it. But that particular morning, as she was looking down at her finger, a call came from Tokyo to tell her the sad news that her mother had just choked to death on some food.

The fact that the daughter was looking at the ring at the very moment her mother passed away made the ring untouchable and therefore it had to be disposed of at any cost. I was very uncomfortable with this horrendous story and did not want the ring back. I had specifically sold it on a non-return basis and even though I could have bought it much below my previous cost, I had to turn my client to a colleague in New York who bought himself what diamontaires call a *METZIAH*, a bargain. Who knows, perhaps one with a curse!

RULE BRITTANIA

For over six centuries British sterling silver has been quality controlled. The hallmark of the lion passant is respected the world over and the silver content at 92.5 percent indicating the sterling standard is universally appreciated.

In 1339, nineteen goldsmiths bought a property in Foster Lane, London, for the use of the Goldsmiths' Company. Though extended in area, this is the identical site on which Goldsmiths' Hall stands today and no other company can claim a longer or earlier tenure.

If you care to visit the basement of Goldsmiths Hall, you may be allowed into the inner sanctum where you will see copper plates with each individual silversmith's registered hallmark, usually his stylized initials, going back for hundreds of years.

Penalties were great for sub-standard silver. These included destruction of the pieces submitted for marking.

In addition to the sterling and maker's marks, there are marks for the city, e.g. an anchor for Birmingham, the year of manufacture, signified by twenty-two letters of the alphabet, and that of the ruling monarch, e.g. George IV.

Because of this rigidly controlled system, British silver is prized like no other. Antique British silver pre-1800 is rare and commands large prices at auction.

Heller Antiques had two very special exhibitions of British Silver.

Here follows the welcoming notice of the first show, which we arranged in association with the British Embassy.

November, 1985

It is a great pleasure to welcome you to our annual Silver Exhibition.

This year we are greatly honored to co-host our Showing with her Britannic Majesty's Ambassador, Sir Oliver Wright.

The timing of our event coincides with "The Treasure Houses of Britain" series, and Washington is indeed fortunate to be custodian of the contents of the some 200 great collections which have crossed the Atlantic.

We are deeply indebted to several friends who are "soulmates" with us in our love of fine silver. They have graciously allowed their silver to be placed on loan for the Exhibition. Alas, security and personal reasons must make them anonymous.

Silver, that precious metal, has inspired craftsmen for millennia. English Silver – Sterling – has for many centuries been a universal standard of quality. The names of Paul de Lamerie and Paul Storr are known to collectors world-wide.

Thanks must also be expressed to our patrons who have allowed our company to grow from strength to strength.

It is therefore with gratitude and pride that we present the exhibits and trust that they will meet with your approval.

The Heller Family

In addition to our own vast stock of quality silver there were forty loan exhibits that were out of this world, including Elizabethan items from the year 1599; a salver on foot, Commonwealth Era, London 1656; a gilt covered porringer cup from the reign of Charles II, London 1660; a Monteith bowl and a two-handled cup from the Queen Anne period 1711; a tea caddy set including three caddies, six spoons and tongs, George II,

London 1730 and my best, the pierced and engraved Beaufort Cake Basket by Paul de Lamerie, London 1740 made for Charles Noel Somerset, the 4th Duke of Beaufort.

Washington never had a private showing of this quality of silver before. The multimillion dollar collection required round the clock security to obtain insurance cover.

For the gala opening, we erected a large marquee on the plaza of the Barlow Building where we had an open bar and a delicious buffet featuring English dishes.

Flanking the entrance were my two beautiful nieces, Susan and Janine Heller, dressed in beefeater costumes.

At the appointed hour, the British Ambassador and his wife arrived in their gleaming Rolls Royce. We were ready to receive Sir Oliver and Lady Wright. The band struck up patriotic English music and we escorted the diplomats into our enlarged emporium. They were a charming couple and showed admiration and knowledge for the exhibits.

Even when one of our elderly clients, an Anglophile, who had gone too far at our pub, came up and gave Lady Wright a strong kiss on the lips, she smiled with much grace.

The show was a hit and made all the newspapers.

A year later we had another exhibition of British Silver, very different from the first. The 1986 show was titled "English Arts and Crafts Silver."

This is the welcoming notice:

C.R. ASHBEE and the GUILD OF HANDICRAFT

Charles Robert Ashbee was born in 1863 into the prosperous English upper bourgeois class.

As a child he embarked upon a modest project which influenced his career – the construction of a large doll's house, big enough for forty dolls. In spite of his attention to detail and his high hopes, the doll's house proved to be unstable and collapsed. This was almost prophetic.

Ashbee became an architect, one of the best known in the English Arts and Crafts movement. He also set out to "reconstruct society." His noble aspirations and lost causes were reflected in the fate of the Guild of Handicraft which was inaugurated in 1888 and liquidated in 1908.

Great emphasis was placed on developing the creative individuality of each workman, and the early years were years of continuous expansion and experiment with a wide range of crafts, including base metalwork, furniture, interior decorating, silver, jewelry and wrought ironwork. This was also an experiment in social democracy.

His wife, Janet, was fascinated by the Guild workshops and became an enthusiastic supporter.

In 1902, the "back-to-the-land" ideology and Ashbee's visionary zeal brought the Guild from Essex House in London to Campden in the Cotswolds. Campden was the ideal socialists' dream city, Ashbee's "City of the Sun."

The Campden School of Arts and Crafts was founded in 1904. Initially, many celebrities patronized the new school, but its success was short-lived. Ashbee moved to other fields. He died in 1942.

Perhaps Ashbee and his Guild were ahead of their time.

We are fortunate to have acquired this important collection which we are offering for sale in its entirety.

The metalwork and enamel collection of Ashbee and his Guild included:

- a hand-beaten copper box with enamel plaque
- pair of menu stands modeled as owls
- decanter bound in silver
- hot-water kettle upon stand
- punch bowl with semi-precious stones
- clock with tapering sides
- trophy with naked figure on domed base

- art nouveau table mirror

Although this was a much smaller exhibition, it was well received and we had museum curators from New York, Richmond, as well as from the local Smithsonian, attend the show.

With these shows, Heller was now recognized as the leading silver dealer in the Washington metropolitan area.

Izzy Heller

L TO R: IZZY, LADY WRIGHT, AMBASSADOR SIR OLIVER WRIGHT AND ZELDA

JANINE AND SUSAN HELLER

Secrets of a Jeweler

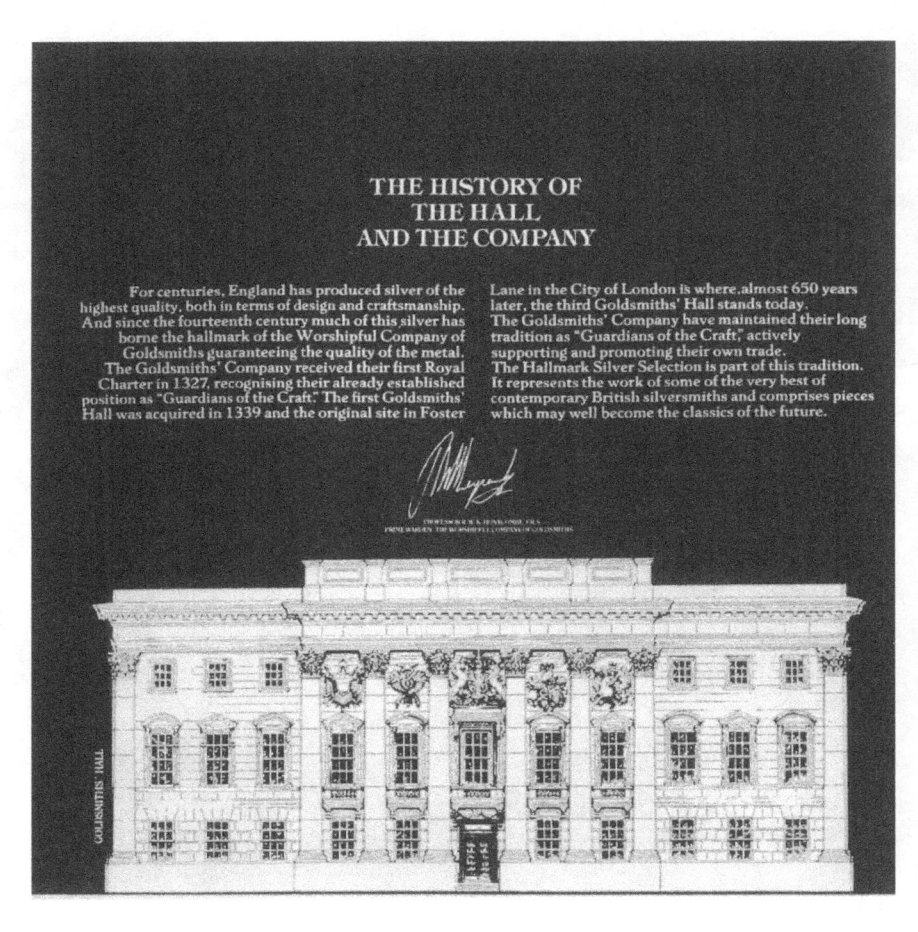

THE HISTORY OF THE HALL AND THE COMPANY

For centuries, England has produced silver of the highest quality, both in terms of design and craftsmanship. And since the fourteenth century much of this silver has borne the hallmark of the Worshipful Company of Goldsmiths guaranteeing the quality of the metal. The Goldsmiths' Company received their first Royal Charter in 1327, recognising their already established position as "Guardians of the Craft." The first Goldsmiths' Hall was acquired in 1339 and the original site in Foster Lane in the City of London is where, almost 650 years later, the third Goldsmiths' Hall stands today. The Goldsmiths' Company have maintained their long tradition as "Guardians of the Craft," actively supporting and promoting their own trade. The Hallmark Silver Selection is part of this tradition. It represents the work of some of the very best of contemporary British silversmiths and comprises pieces which may well become the classics of the future.

FAÇADE OF GOLDSMITHS' HALL

Izzy Heller

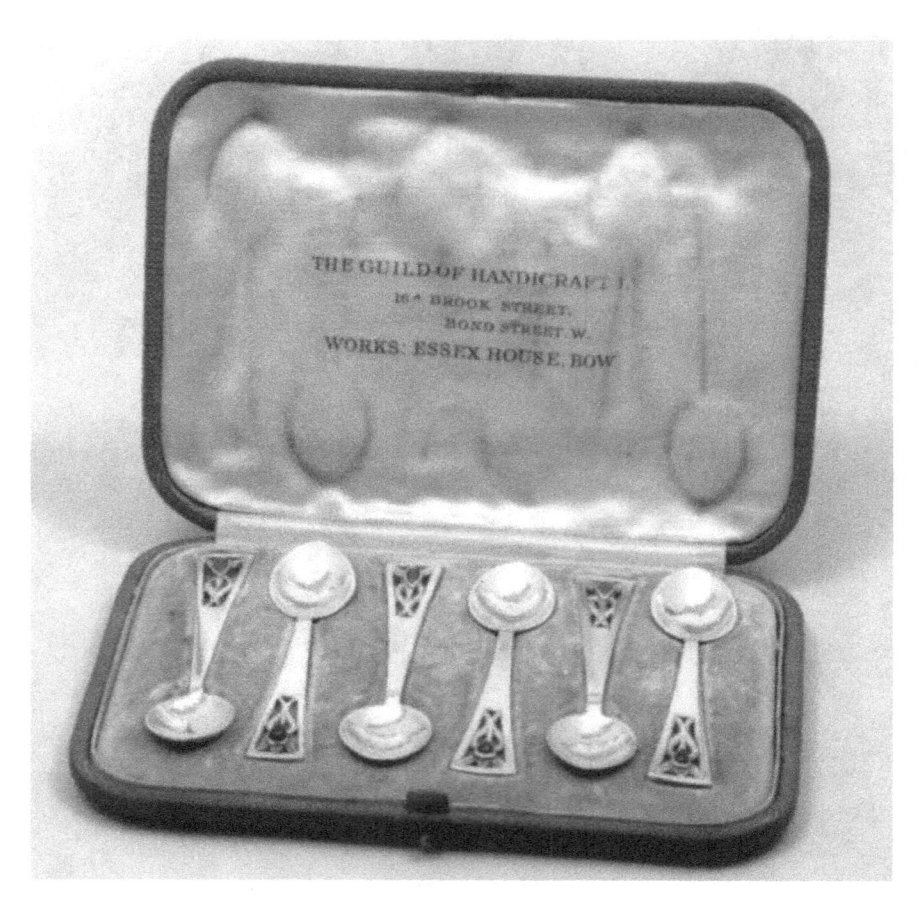

ENGLISH SILVER SPOONS FROM THE ARTS AND CRAFTS PERIOD

Secrets of a Jeweler

ENGLISH SILVER KETTLE FROM THE ARTS AND CRAFTS PERIOD

Izzy Heller

ONE OF OUR SILVER ADS

MAKING WAVES

Verizon SuperPages claims to be "the best advertising value in the Washington, D.C. Metro Area."

The very same is boasted by the newspapers, magazines, TV channels and radio stations operating in this region. And each submits statistics (remember the saying "lies, damn lies and statistics") to prove their point.

The high advertising rates of the *Washington Post* the dominant – some say the only – newspaper seem to go up each year. So do the prices of most other media purchases, especially in radio, where the number of independents has dropped dramatically with the urge to merge. Here there are fifty radio stations with probably eight owners.

So how does a little retailer decide where to allocate very limited resources to get a message across a segment of this population?

In my case, by trial and error. A very expensive method, but I became so hardened and cynical by the high-powered twisted presentations of the media sales "executives" that I could think of no other path to take. Their expertise was what the politicians call SPIN.

Our experience showed we got more "Bang For The Buck" from selective radio advertising than from Verizon, *Washington Post*, *Washingtonian Magazine*, Cable TV, *The Gazette* etc, etc.

We made enquiries and were pointed in the direction of a fancy Madison Avenue agency for producing radio commercials. But we did not think their proposals were right for Heller Jewelers. Too impersonal, too slick. I wanted something that reinforced our being a family business, that we had names and faces and delivered good honest value and personal service.

So we prepared our own radio commercials. I worked on a jingle and came up with a catchy tune with a happy vocal and this became our standard musical DONUT for our messages across the sound waves.

The word DONUT in radio parlance refers to the jingle introducing and ending the sixty second spot, leaving the middle of the time slot for our text messaging, which invariably involved a little chit-chat between Zelda and me.

To sell fine estate jewelry is far easier than to purchase the same. Therefore our advertising dollars went to spreading the word that HELLER BUYS.

The production of each of our radio spots involved a trip to Rockville where Doug Stevens, our guru, had set up shop. He is the president of Back Trax.

Doug is a muscular, stocky, earringed Harley-Davidson fan. He is also a genius in the field of radio commercials and "on hold" phone messaging.

Initially it would take Zelda and me several hours in Doug's studio to prepare a commercial. Within six months, we had it down to one hour.

We would alternate occupancy of a tiny sound booth and read our piece – sometimes a dozen times, before I approved – and Doug would then put our voices where they belonged, all within the DONUT.

Here follows a sampling five texts of our radio ads.

RADIO AD – "M.O." – AUGUST 1996

Announcer: We're in Chevy Chase with Zelda, wife of Izzy Heller of Heller Jewelers. Is it true? Does Izzy have an "M.O." for buying diamonds?

Zelda: Absolutely. His "Mad Obsession" to acquire diamonds is a compulsion. What can he possibly do with thousands of diamonds? Just listen to him.

Izzy: My love of diamonds may enable you to fulfill your dreams. The answer to a wish often starts in the sale of diamonds to Heller Jewelers. We have the money for the things you want and now may be a good time to sell. Perhaps you could use the cash right now.

Secrets of a Jeweler

Zelda: Purchasing diamonds is Izzy's mission in life. He doesn't stop.

Izzy: Heller Jewelers offers top prices for almost any diamonds, jewelry or silver brought for sale.

Zelda: He's driven. He goes on and on. He even repeats himself.

Izzy: I offer excellent prices and immediate payment, with my personal guarantee of fair treatment and the utmost confidentiality.

Zelda: Diamonds are his best friend. His "M.O." is with diamonds. He's focused. He's committed. Hear him again.

Izzy: Yes, I want to buy your diamonds! See Heller, a name you can trust. Heller, 5454 Wisconsin Avenue at Friendship Heights Metro. Call 1-800-78 H.E. Double L. E. R.

RADIO AD – "BANKER" – APRIL 1997

Announcer: We're in Chevy Chase with Izzy Heller of Heller Jewelers. Izzy, why do people think of you as a banker?

Izzy: Because "cash right now" is our slogan. We supply instant liquidity for diamonds, jewelry and silver.

Announcer: Doesn't everyone pay right now?

Izzy: No they don't. Auction Houses don't. And their hammer price is not your price. Consignment firms don't. When they say "Maybe and tomorrow," it's not money in your pocket.

Announcer: If I come to Heller, do I stand in line? Complete an application form?

Izzy: No, the process is simple. We evaluate your diamonds and jewelry fairly and quickly and make you a free offer. No pressure. Absolutely private. Upon acceptance, we give you a check.

Announcer: How do your clients react when they sell to you and what do

	they do with the money they get from Heller?
Izzy:	Their smiles speak for them when they take our checks. For we've given them excellent prices and money for the things they want – a cruise, a car or the relief of paying Uncle Sam.
Announcer:	So if you have diamonds or jewelry for sale and can use the cash right now, see Heller – a name you can trust. Heller, 5454 Wisconsin Avenue. Call 1-800-78-HELLER.

RADIO AD – "EXERCISE" – MARCH 2000

Izzy:	Hi! I'm Izzy Heller of Heller Jewelers, Chevy Chase. As you may know, I'm an energetic buyer of diamonds, fine jewelry and silver.
Zelda:	"Exercise is good for you" I keep telling my husband.
Izzy:	If you have jewelry and diamonds gathering dust, bring them to Heller Jewelers now. Don't delay. Perhaps you can use the cash right now.
Zelda:	This is what he says: "I don't have the strength to walk on a treadmill. It's torture."
Izzy:	Since 1957, my family has been buying diamonds and jewelry. I treasure our reputation built on courtesy, fair pricing and immediate payment. We have the money for the things you want and now may be a good time to sell. I love the smile when you take my check. So come on in.
Zelda:	Tell Izzy there's a diamond sale miles away and suddenly he becomes a marathon runner. I suppose that's what keeps him young.
Announcer:	If you have diamonds or jewelry for sale see Heller. A name you can trust. Heller 5454 Wisconsin Avenue. 1-800-78-HELLER.

RADIO AD – "SUMMER VACATION" – APRIL 2002

Izzy: Hi! I'm Izzy Heller of Heller Jewelers, Chevy Chase. Let <u>me</u> pay for your summer vacation this year.

Zelda: Isn't my husband in a generous mood!

Izzy: The money I give you for unwanted jewelry and diamonds may take you to Aspen, The Hamptons, or wherever. So come into Heller Jewelers right now.

Zelda: Big talker: He's really a stay-at-home. <u>I'd</u> like us to visit Rome, Paris and London.

Izzy: Since 1957, my family has been buying diamonds, jewelry and silver. I treasure our reputation, which has been built on courtesy, fair pricing and immediate payment. We have the money for the things you want and now may be a good time to sell. I love the smile when you take my check. So come on in.

Zelda: If Izzy keeps on with this constant diamond buying, I'm taking my vacation on the Falkland Islands!

Announcer: So if you have diamonds or jewelry for sale, see Heller. A name you can trust. Heller, 5454 Wisconsin Avenue, Chevy Chase call 1-800-78-HELLER

RADIO AD – "ARNOLD SCHWARZ-A-NAME" – SEPTEMBER 2002

Izzy: Hi! I'm Izzy Heller of Heller Jewelers, Chevy Chase. Fine jewelry and exquisite gems are my passion and finding these treasures is my business.

Zelda: I said to Izzy: You can't keep going at this pace. You've got to slow down. Let's go to Europe and relax.

Izzy: I will go anywhere in the world to buy diamonds and jewelry. If you're far or near, contact Heller Jewelers. Perhaps you can use the cash right now.

Zelda: So we go to London, Vienna, Budapest. And he's buying again! He's obsessed with discovering beautiful things.

Izzy: Since 1957 my family has been buying diamonds and jewelry. I treasure our reputation, which has been built on courtesy, fair pricing and immediate payment. Now may be a good time to sell. I love the smile when you take my check. So come on in.

Zelda: If Izzy used all that energy on the treadmill, he'd have a build like Arnold Schwarz-a-name!

Announcer: So if you have jewelry for sale, see Heller a name you can trust. Heller, 5454 Wisconsin Avenue, Chevy Chase. call 1-800-78-HELLER.

This last ad may have made Arnold famous. Who would have thought that Schwarznegger would become Governor of California?

Our campaign was a stunning success! More and more people visited our store and we attracted just the target audience we sought – people with fine diamonds and spectacular jewelry to sell.

They quoted from our radio commercials. They asked: Who's Izzy? Where's Zelda? They hummed our jingle. What a response! We were making waves on the air.

My voice, country South African, is very distinctive to Americans, which I imagine was a plus when we advertised on the radio. But sometimes the instant voice recognition of Izzy Heller was a bit much.

I'll always remember getting into a cab at National Airport one evening after a hard day's work in New York. "I'd like to go to Wisconsin Avenue in Chevy Chase please," I told the driver. He was already pulling away at high speed from the rank, when he turned round to me and laughed: "You're Izzy!" he said it as if he had just deciphered the Rosetta Stone.

One evening, Zelda and I were having dinner at a little Italian restaurant in Bethesda when we observed a woman at the next table obviously eavesdropping on our conversation. When confronted with my eye-contact, she sheepishly asked, "Are you on TV?" My wife, a veteran trouble-maker, nodded. The woman, who recognized my voice but could not place it, handed me a white napkin to autograph.

She seemed pleased with the two words I scrawled – "Michael Caine."

Zelda and I made a quick getaway.

LADIES, LADIES EVERYWHERE

In 1985, five years after our arrival as immigrants, we became proud citizens of the U.S.A. It was a day we will always remember. We shed a lot of happy tears on that day.

It started early in the Courthouse downtown, where a Judge officiated and presented us with our certificates after officials delivered moving, patriotic speeches. There were 112 of us. All we had to do was take the oath of allegiance together and then announce our country of birth individually. We were the only South Africans, but it seemed that every other country was represented. We knew what we had gone through. We could only imagine the sufferings of some of those new Americans. What a great country this is!

The ceremony concluded with a short address by an official of the Daughters of the American Revolution (D.A.R.) – decorated with a colorful diagonal ribbon across her chest - who invited us to have refreshments in an adjoining lounge. There we were warmly received and everyone relaxed after the tension of the formalities. I am always grateful to the D.A.R. for that party and for Linda and Hershel Katz for attending.

We returned to our office with our large, freshly embossed and colorful Certificates of Naturalization and there we found Nancy, our manager, had prepared home-made ice cream with freshly baked apple pie. If that was not enough, the place was decorated in red, white and blue and we were given coffee-table books of various beautiful areas of America.

To round off the wonderful day, our friends gave us a surprise party, a kind of "This Is Your Life." The organizers had researched our family's history and presented it in rhyme to popular music. There were costumes, dances and fun to cap the evening. We knew no American for more than five years, so the fellowship which was recent meant a lot to us.

Several years later, I was privileged to meet Mrs. Taylor who had the unusual first and middle names of May and Day. May Day Taylor had a successful business known as United Buying Service. She was also a big

Secrets of a Jeweler

shot in the D.A.R. and invited me to view the library of the organization, housed in a fabulous building near the White House.

The library with its upstairs gallery is magnificent and I was impressed not only with their books and records but also with their collection of Americana.

A Centennial Tea was being planned for the anniversary of Dolley Madison's birthday on May 20. I learned that Dolley's "unfailing accessory of every dress was her snuff box . . . smart ladies cultivated the habit. The women liked her as much as the men . . . that she snuffed was further evidence of her open honesty."

I acquired an early American silver snuff box and immediately offered it as a gift to the D.A.R. Museum. Remembering the citizenship party, it was the least I could do.

For my donation, I was invited to the Centennial Tea. I was the only male in the presence of 200 women formally dressed – all with colorful ribbons. When I arrived, May Day welcomed me and told me the good news that I would be one of the speakers. Luckily, I was not intimidated and the tea and my talk all went down well.

Izzy Heller

The Dolley Madison Chapter Centennial Tea
May 20, 1992
On the Anniversary of Dolley Madison's Birthday
The Thomas Law House, District of Columbia

Greeting you in the Receiving Line are Mrs. Edward R. Lang, *Honorary Chapter Regent*; Mr. and Mrs. James Madison (Cmdr. and Mrs. James R. Sowers); Mrs. Martha S. Galbreath, *Chapter Regent* and Mrs. Gary L. Guidotti, *District of Columbia DAR State Librarian*.
Refreshments are being served on the first floor and upstairs.
Period music is provided by David Moore, Mary Pixley and Nanette Melnick.
Anniversary Remarks: Mrs. May Day Taylor, *Past Vice President General*
Greetings: Mrs. Ferris L. French, *State Regent*
Introductions: Mr. and Mrs. Richard Bland Lee (Mr. and Mrs. Michael J. McInerney), *close friends of the Madisons*; Mrs. Gary R. Meeds, *Corresponding Secretary General NSDAR*; Mrs. Robert A. Bier, *59 year member* and Mrs. Ardis W. Finnamore, *Chapter Biographer of Dolley.*
The serving of Dolley's cake and her "favorite sweet," ice cream!

Built in 1784, this handsome Federalist mansion at the corner of Sixth and N Streets, S.W., has been the home and social center for some of the city's leading figures. In 1796, its mistress was Elizabeth Parke Custis, the spirited eldest granddaughter of the First Lady, Martha Washington. As a young bride, Eliza was brought here to live by her husband Thomas Law, Esquire, aristocrat and brother to Lord Ellenborough, the Lord Chief Justice of England. The mansion subsequently became famous as the "Honeymoon House" and was the scene of many a brilliant party to which guests came by coach or often by boat from Alexandria and Georgetown. Mrs. Law boasted of the best kitchen in Washington and her hospitality was generous and informal. Soon, however, Dr. Thornton reported "the joys of housekeeping no longer awaited to relieve the tedium of a life with a boring husband" and Mr. and Mrs. Law provided Washington with a real scandal: a divorce. (While the Laws lived so elegantly, the Madisons, to avoid the taint of land speculators, rented less spacious quarters from Elbridge Gerry.) "In the readjustments which followed the breakup of the Law establishment, with its faultless stove, its graceful curtains and its stock of books going in various directions, Mrs. Madison received her share." Years later, the house was purchased by Richard Bland Lee.

Dolley's "unfailing accessary of every dress was her snuff box . . . smart ladies cultivated the habit." The women liked her as much as the men . . . "that she 'rouged' and 'snuffed' was merely further evidence of her open honesty." Our snuff box is provided by Heller Antiques, Ltd. and presented by Thomas Taylor. Handkerchiefs were as essential as snuff and Dolley carried two, one for show and one for the "rough stuff." Our handkerchiefs today are donated by the chapter members to honor Dolley and the 358 women who have been members of the chapter.

Dolley's rescue of the portrait of George Washington is legendary. In the face of British troops advancing on the city, she sent French John back to the President's House to bank the kitchen fires, lock the doors and get her parrot to safety. "This little pet was Dolley's great treasure" and she kept it beside her for many years. We thank Orva G. Clubb for bringing her parrot to this party.

Dolley's Portrait is hanging in this house today through the courtesy of the District of Columbia DAR State Regent and the Chapter House Committee.
The flowers are arranged by Mary Lee Bolte. The man-servant at the front door is Scott Shewmaker.
The Dolley Madison Chapter DAR Centennial Certificate is on display with other chapter memorabilia. Enjoy!

D.A.R. PROGRAM

Secrets of a Jeweler

SILVER SNUFF BOX PRESENTED BY IZZY TO THE D.A.R. MUSEUM

THE DDC OF NYC

"If you can make it here, you can make it anywhere" goes the song about New York, New York. I feel that is certainly true.

New York is the center of things. Over half the diamonds sold in the U.S. goes through hands around one street block, West 47th Street between 5th and 6th Avenues. There appears to be limitless liquidity, unlimited demand there – all if one's price is low!

In an attempt to gain entry into that lucrative market, I "cold-called" on hundreds of dealers and after a few years could count perhaps two dozen regular accounts. Rejection comes with the territory and one cannot be tender-skinned to trade in Manhattan.

It is a tough market to crack and it was physically hard on me to work the street without a home base, which I eventually established at the DDC of NYC.

The Diamond Dealers Club is housed in a skyscraper on the corner of Fifth Avenue and West 47th Street in New York City. The building is called five-eighty, the Avenue number. However, the Club's entrance is on 47th.

The DDC occupies 2 floors in the building. The Club's offices are situated on the 11th floor. On the 10th, in addition to the restaurants, there is a news room (TV's, bulletin boards, newspapers), room of meditation and worship (mainly Jewish), a games room (cards, chess and backgammon) a message center, a weigh and grade cubicle, booths of telephones, a manned coat room, personal lockers, toilets and oh yes, a trading floor for diamonds. This latter section consists of rows of tables and chairs with diamond lights.

Membership of the Club does not come easily, quickly or cheaply. A very detailed application form must be submitted accompanied by three sponsorships, personal financial details, a business history, photograph and a big check. A few months later, a personal interview before the membership committee is required. By this time, the applicant will have been checked out at every diamond bourse in the world since the DDC is part of the World Federation of Diamond Bourses. One blemish and you're out.

To serve on any committee of the DDC is an honor but the highest regard is for the members of the Arbitration Committee. They are the judges.

DDC members, 99 percent of whom are honorable, nonetheless get themselves involved in disputes with other members. Membership in the DDC obligates each member to settle any disputes with any other member through the DDC's Arbitration tribunals. No member may go to any outside court system for resolution of complaints with another member unless the Club's Arbitration system expressly grants that permission. Arbitrators have the power to subpoena, fine and suspend members who do not abide by their decisions.

State and Federal courts have consistently upheld the DDC's jurisdiction and the decisions of its Arbitration Tribunals.

Security is paramount at the Club. Uniformed and plain-clothed officials are all over. Metal detectors, cameras – you name it. Access is severely limited and carefully controlled.

Although there is no sex discrimination, this is a man's club. I have seen only one woman trader on the floor. Her regular position is in the left hand front corner. In that culture, she seems to "know her place." There is a requirement of maintaining an atmosphere of professionalism with businesslike behavior. There is a dress code. For women this includes modesty, the prohibition of short skirts, sleeveless and low cut attire. For men, a jacket is required. Sneakers are banned. Two concepts are common in the trading practices at the DDC – the use of a CACHET and the practice of MEMORANDUM. Let me elaborate on these everyday usages.

A CACHET is a sealed envelope in which a prospective buyer has placed a stone(s). The CACHET precludes the viewing of the sealed goods by anyone other than the prospective buyer. An offered price and any terms that may be desired can be written on the CACHET which constitutes an offer by the buyer.

A CACHET is valid for 24 hours (or one full working day) when sealed by a New York buyer, and up to 48 hours (two working days) when the prospective buyer is out of New York and the transaction is handled by a BROKER in New York.

Sending out merchandise on consignment is a common practice in the jewelry trade and results in millions of dollars of business monthly. Goods so sent can be designated as MEMORANDUM (MEMO). The items listed on the MEMO become the consignee's financial, legal and ethical responsibility from the moment the MEMO is signed. Such goods are "lent" to the consignee for possible sale and may not be pledged, nor can they in any way leave the possession of the consignee without the owner's explicit consent. The goods remain the property of the owner until a transaction is completed. Goods on MEMORANDUM may be recalled at the discretion of the owner. Goods must be returned promptly upon demand by the owner.

The rules of memo trading appear to be clear. Yet the issues surrounding memo deliveries are complex, thereby making fraud difficult to prosecute. A majority of the disputes at the DDC relate to memos.

Richard Maslin, a jeweler in Beverly Hills, California pawned memo goods to help with his financial problems and never paid the consignor. This was successfully prosecuted and Maslin was sent to jail. Through experiences like this, diamond suppliers are doing more thorough credit checks before sending out on memo.

I enjoyed being a member of the DDC. Often I would take the Delta or U.S.Air Shuttle from Washington's Reagan National to New York's La Guardia at the crack of dawn and arrive by cab at the Club soon after it opened. On the 10th floor apart from the restaurant, there is also a food counter with bar stools. There I would catch my breath, have my bagel and cream cheese with a decaf before starting the hectic day.

One such morning in winter when the bitter cold had all of us wearing coat, gloves, scarf and hat – a damn nuisance when one was in and out of elevators – I got up from my breakfast alongside several orthodox Chassidic Jews to see several flutes on the floor nearby. A flute consists of several sheets of special paper folded in a prescribed way so that the diamond contents would be safe.

The flutes on the floor were bulging. I could not believe my eyes. One of my friends was probably so busy with the protective clothing that the packets must have fallen.

I gathered the 4 parcel papers, glanced at the writing on the outside folds: 12.57 carats, 16.81 carats, 9.55 carats, 11.29 carats. My curiosity got the better of me and I folded back the cover of one flute. Colorless beauties were present. I made my way to the Head of Security and told him what I had found. I was required to give a written report. A director of the DDC was summoned. By this time a crowd had gathered, and one bearded guy was shouting "It's mine! It's mine!" He too was asked for a written report. He rattled off the numbers: 12.57 carats round, 16.81 carats rounds, 9.55 carats pears, 11.29 carats princess. Probably, all in all, a value of some $60,000. He was given his merchandise but not allowed to move. His fellow members surrounded him and were chanting *TZEDAKEH! TZEDAKEH!* (Charity! Charity!). Only when he had pledged $1,000 to a worthy cause, was the lucky trader free to move.

This place was my branch office in New York City. I felt secure. I had a locker. I had a place I could store my suitcase. And I was in the heart of the action. New Yorkers are not bashful. The traders would elbow their way to me. "What you got?" they would bark. In a ruthless business environment where a percentage point can be a deal-breaker, I met some of my better clients and did some of my biggest deals high up in Manhattan, at the DDC.

WHAT'S IT WORTH?

With ownership often comes the perception of great value. After all, Granny said that the tea service was hand-made by a great Russian silversmith in the 1600's. Never mind that the markings bore the punch of the American company, Rogers, that the A1 referred to electroplate-over-nickel and that the style was early 20th Century. It's hard to tell the owner that the cash value of the set is a mere $200 after Granny had come down from the Mount.

To estimate value, one needs an independent appraiser, one who is schooled in appraising law and discipline and who has training and experience in the specific field of operation. Real property of course relates to land, bricks and mortar. Personal property covers inter alia, jewelry and silver. Appraisers should charge on the basis of time, not on value, to avoid a conflict of interest.

Since appraising is not a licensed profession, one should only appoint an appraiser who is a member of one of these organizations:

The International Society of Appraisers

1131 SW Seventh Street, Suite 105

Renton, WA 98055

206.241.0359 www.isa-appraisers.org

The American Society of Appraisers

555 Herndon Parkway, Suite 125

Herndon, VA 20170

703.478.2228 . www.appraisers.org

The National Association of Jewelry Appraisers

PO Box 18

Rego Park, NY 11374

718.896.1536

The American Gem Society Laboratory (AGSL)

8917 West Sahara Avenue

Las Vegas, NV 89117

702.223.6120 www.agslab.com

The value of an item can vary substantially for different types of appraisals. For example a "forced sale" valuation to determine collateral for a bank will be much lower than an insurance valuation for "replacement value, new."

United States law encourages charity so contributions can be deducted from taxable income. Likewise, the law prescribes that inheritances are taxed. In both these cases, charitable contributions and estate transfers, appraisers are called upon for certification. Advocacy rears its ugly head in these matters. It is not ethical to go with "suggested" values to suit the client's needs. The donor, in the case of the contribution, wants as high a value as possible, the beneficiary, in an estate situation, wants as low a value as possible. Alas, both voices are heard by the appraiser. The law is clear and fair. In both these cases, the same basis is used by the Internal Revenue Service and fair market value between a willing buyer and willing seller is defined in the statute and tested in court.

Recently a federal tax probe focused on the donation and value of four Stradivarius string instruments donated to the Smithsonian Institution by Herbert R. Axelrod, who claimed they were worth $50 million. Was this a generous contribution or a method to beat the I.R.S.? Axelrod fled to Cuba to avoid tax charges and then made his was to Germany, where he was arrested. The case of the fiddler is still ongoing.

The most common appraisal is the Insurance Appraisal, generally intended to cover the owner for loss by replacement of the item.

Jewelry is frequently sold at discounted prices and the vendors often issue appraisal certificates at the pre-discounted higher prices. This is wrong on two counts. Ethically the seller of an item cannot also be its appraiser. This is not an arms-length transaction. The seller can however, issue an "insurance report" giving a detailed description and the actual net price paid. When the jeweler "puffs" an insurance appraisal, the client pays a premium based on that higher value. If there is a claim, the client may not get payment for that higher value, usually because the insurer has an option to replace the item "with like or similar" and can do that for much less than the inflated value.

The history of prior ownership or provenance can have an enormous effect on the value of an item. With its provenance, the simulated pearl necklace of Jacqueline Kennedy Onassis was sold in New York in 1996 for $211,500. Without that ownership, the necklace "would be worth" about $200.

Auction records abound with examples of large premiums being paid for personality pieces. The Duchess of Windsor had a lovely collection of jewelry but the prices realized by her estate were several times the normal values.

I'll never forget the day we received a call from a client to help her driver unload the jewelry at the curbside outside our store. The valuables were to be appraised for insurance purposes.

A few minutes later the chauffeur pulled up, and we were waiting with our cart. Several trips later, we had transferred the 8 footlockers into the safety of our store. Before we knew it, the car had left.

A rule in our industry prescribes that we issue a detailed receipt for every single thing received, be it $50 or $5,000. Certainly if the value is $5 million! That's what the contents of the footlockers were worth! And no list had been given and no receipt had been issued. What if the client claimed that there were additional items not accounted for?

I immediately called the owner and explained my concern. Her relaxed response was "I trust you."

Three of us were present when every single item was checked and documented. The appraisal took over a month to complete. I was pleased and relieved when it was over. The responsibility was almost too much. We called and asked for the 8 footlockers to be picked up. Sure, she said, and we'll deliver the rest at the same time! Again no list when another $3 million arrived and this time we insisted that the driver be present at take-in.

Secrets of a Jeweler

After completion of our work on this lot, we were told to return the jewelry to the owner's home. The housekeeper came to the door, said Madam was busy and would we just leave it near the umbrella stand!

There is great wealth in the Washington, D.C. metro area. Residents have inherited real estate fortunes, but great personal treasures have also been handed down from estates all over the world. As an appraiser, it has been my good fortune to have handled hundreds of museum quality items even though it has been a challenge to answer the frequently asked question: "WHAT'S IT WORTH?"

HARRY THE PLUNDERER

Nothing about Harry was small. He was taller than me which made him over six feet. He was very much heavier than me, probably 270 pounds. He had a moustache and bearded chin and wore big horn-rimmed spectacles. Harry E. Kingston was black and bejeweled. I reckon he was in his forties and he reminded me of Mr. T.

It was a Saturday afternoon in April, 1988 when the limo pulled up outside 5454 Wisconsin Avenue. Harry alighted and was escorted by a young white teenager into our store.

The unusual appearance of Mr. Kingston caused much excitement. The activity of our customers froze. Conversation stopped. The staring could not be contained, but this did not faze our new client one bit. He asked to speak to the owner.

With great charm, he introduced himself as a banker from Chicago, who had a home off Embassy Row/Massachusetts Avenue, D.C. He was here on a short visit but felt a little naked, as the 9 rings on his fingers left his pinky unclothed. We both laughed.

Let me digress for a moment. My father's cousin, Seymour Heller of Hollywood, California had been the great Liberace's manager for over 30 years. On the performer's death, Seymour sent us some items of jewelry gifted to him by Liberace for which he had no use. He shipped them on consignment for us to sell. One such ring had a circle with a revolving diamond, like a roulette wheel. I had promised a bonus to whoever sold this goddam awful piece of jewelry. It was so ugly, we could not display it. To Harry's credit, he dismissed the ring when I showed it to him. I had under-estimated him.

He found his ring among the ruby selection. It had a 2 carat blood red stone of fine quality in an oval shape surrounded by 2 rows of fine diamonds. It was a regular lady's finger size, a six. We measured his pinky. It took a size 11 ½, almost double the circumference of our ring shank. To increase by that much is no easy task, even for a master jeweler, who had to exercise great care not to destabilize the stones. To complicate matters,

Secrets of a Jeweler

Kingston wanted the ring for a party he was giving that very evening. He asked me to deliver it in person so he could show me his lovely "second home." Harry paid for the $15,000 purchase with a platinum American Express card.

At 5:30pm when I knocked on the door of the mansion on California Street, N.W., it was Wilson the butler who escorted me into the study to await his master's arrival.

By then Harry and I were on first name terms and when he saw the ring fit beautifully on his finger, we became hugging buddies.

Over a couple of whiskeys, Harry told me that he had grown up in a slum neighborhood of Chicago. He was gifted with a fine voice but turned down a job with the New York Metropolitan Opera, because he feared he would become a starving artist. So he attended a local college. His first jobs were modest: a waiter and then a trainee at a local bank.

In 1970 he somehow got a management position and later the Presidency at Universal Community Federal Credit Union, a small struggling local institution.

Well-meaning nonprofit entities helped Universal with low-cost funds. Charities held millions in certificates of deposit from Universal. Likewise local business leaders and the local newspaper, the Chicago World-Herald, were ardent supporters of the Credit Union which professed to help the poor.

Universal Community appeared to thrive and so did Mr. Kingston. He became a role model in the black community. His white Mercedes and four-story mansion were known to all. His wealth and prominence were seen as a beacon of hope. He defended his lavish life style as an indication that hard work pays off.

The city of Chicago showed its appreciation for his hard work by showering him with honors. His investments now included restaurants and a landscaping company.

Harry became active in the Republican Party. As a large contributor, he was asked to sing the national anthem at the 1984 opening ceremony of the National Convention. Later he hosted a lavish party at Southfork Ranch, where the TV show *Dallas* was filmed.

From time to time for eight months since our first meeting, Harry would pop in to say hi. He never disappointed us. The platinum Amex card was hard at work.

The letter addressed to me and hand-delivered was dated November 11, 1988. It read as follows:

Dear Mr. Heller:

> I have asked my representative, Mr. Douglas D. Hasson, to facilitate the sale of some of my jewelry and fine silver items. He should present to you the Power of Attorney personally executed by me authorizing him to engage in the sale and transfer of these items and the authority to execute the proper documents.
>
> Please extend Mr. Hasson every courtesy which you have so kindly extended to me in the past.
>
> Very truly yours
>
> Signed

Harry E. Kingston.

I was surprised that Harry now wished to dispose of his collection and told Mr. Hasson so. Mr. Kingston was going through a cash-flow problem, was the reply and he wanted my best cash offer.

I explained that I would first have to evaluate the items and we would have to agree on price, with payment taking place after the 18 days waiting period as required by law. Mr. Hasson asked if there was a way to get a check sooner. I promised to apply for an "early release" by the police. He agreed and I studied the pieces and made an offer which he promptly accepted. I immediately submitted a detailed report of my purchase and application for quick approval to Montgomery County Police.

It did not take more than 24 hours for the F.B.I. to pay me a visit and inform me that Kingston's success was a sham and that Universal Credit

Union had been closed down by regulators after they discovered some $39 million was missing. At the time, the institution's collapse was the second largest credit union failure ever. They seized Mr. Kingston's collection. In the lawsuit filed, Mr. Kingston was charged with plundering Universal to finance his flamboyant life style. Personal expenses of $1.1 million were charged to an American Express card. All this, while Mr. Kingston earned $20,000 a year as head of the credit union.

The scandal stunned Chicago, despite the fact that most depositors got their money back because of a federal insurance fund.

In 1991 Mr. Kingston pleaded guilty to charges of conspiracy, embezzlement and making false statements. His wife, Joan, entered a guilty plea to the charge of filing a false tax return.

Crime doesn't pay but I couldn't help thinking: Such a nice guy to go to prison....

ARABIAN NIGHT

Although I had been told that every person in Saudi Arabia is either a Royal or related to one, it was a big deal for me to have the Prince and Princess as customers.

I often wondered why they patronized me so often and so generously, knowing I was Jewish. And why they would never look me in the eye or speak to me directly.

All communication – the appointments, the requests, the selections, the negotiations and the payments – were done via their efficient secretary.

She set the time, sometimes during business hours, sometimes after. When required, we would close the store to the public so that we could give them undivided attention.

On one occasion the secretary called late one afternoon to say Her Highness would like to see a selection of earrings and necklaces at the Ritz Carlton, Pentagon City in Northern Virginia as soon as possible. I told my staff to stop what they were doing and assist me with the selection of earrings and necklaces. Soon we were up to $1 million in value, so I needed my son-in-law, Sam, to be an escort in the car behind me. Sam was fluent in Arabic.

When we arrived at the Ritz, we were shown to a special high-security elevator which took us to the penthouse suite, probably all of 5,000 square feet, luxuriously furnished. We were received in a large waiting area next to a bar and presented with the hotel menu. It was difficult to reconcile the alcoholic display with the abstinence we had heard about. We ordered tuna sandwiches and coffee, which we enjoyed, and then waited. And waited. All the time, cradling the million in jewelry. With us, waiting, were the chauffeurs, the hairdressers and a group from Lockheed Martin.

After some 2 hours we were shown in to a conference room where the secretary met us. We exhibited our jewels on a large table. Soon the Princess arrived and with a nod to us proceeded to examine our selection, putting various items aside. She then gave a brief comment in Arabic to her secretary and withdrew. We were told that she would purchase the selected items but also that she now wanted to see rings, bracelets and pins.

I called my office to prepare a new assortment and sent Sam back. The Saudis graciously insisted on sending Sam in their limousine for the pickup.

The new inventory was well received and the final total was substantial. A State Department certificate of exemption from sales tax was presented and we were paid in bundles of $100 bills.

It was late that night when we packed up our goodies and the secretary accompanied us to the elevator. There she presented Sam and me with generous gifts from the Princess.

All in all, an Arabian night to remember.

SAINT ROBERT, the gentile ZIONIST

"One hates to put the book down" was the treasured endorsement by Robert St. John of *DEADLY TRUTH*, a novel I co-authored.

The 100-year life of Robert St. John (1902-2003) is so remarkable that it has been documented hundreds of times. Terry Horowitz, an accomplished author, spent several years writing his biography.

Robert grew up in Chicago and served his country abroad in the U.S. Navy during World War I. On returning home, he won a scholarship to Trinity College in Hartford, Connecticut. He left college to work on the *Hartford Courant* Newspaper before joining the *Chicago Daily News* as a reporter. He and his brother then bought the *Cicero Tribune* in Cicero, Illinois. Their newspaper ran a sensational story about the "business" Al Capone was running. Capone ordered him "disposed of." Robert was beaten up by gangsters and left for dead on a curbside. He was hospitalized and recovered. His career subsequently took him to the *Philadelphia Record* and newspapers in New York City.

In August, 1939, at the start of World War II, St. John left for Europe to become the Balkan correspondent for the Associated Press. While traveling on a Greek troop train, it was strafed by a Nazi plane. He was left with bullets in his legs. He was an eye witness to the entrance of the German forces as they stormed into Romania. Present during the Bucharest pogroms (the slaughter of hundreds of Jews by the Iron Guard), St. John managed to hide a Jewish family in his house and save them from imminent extermination.

The persecution of Jews instilled in him a deep interest in Jewish issues and anti-Semitism. "I realized that I had been born into a group that had been doing this sort of thing for 2000 years and therefore had to bear some of the responsibility," he stated.

Back in New York, St. John joined NBC where on June 6, 1944, he broadcast the news of the D-Day invasion by the Allies. As the troops poured onto the shores of Normandy, he voiced the historical events. "This is the invasion of Hitler's Europe in the fight against Axis aggression."

Secrets of a Jeweler

He reported the dropping of the atomic bomb on Hiroshima in 1945 and soon after was at the NBC microphone for a marathon 72 hours to announce VJ day after the Japanese signed the surrender documents.

Robert St. John traveled to the Middle East and covered the birth of Israel in 1948 and the other wars of 1956, 1967, 1973 and 1982. His intimate knowledge of the region resulted in several books. *Shalom Means Peace* was an account of Israel's creation. He wrote several biographies including those of Ben-Gurion, Ben-Yehuda and Abba Eban.

Robert St. John has been described time and again as nothing less than a renaissance man, having had a distinguished career of over 70 years in journalism, as a celebrated author of 22 books, as a foreign correspondent and lecturer. His devotion to morals and the freedom of the press is legendary.

But it was his biography on the South African Prime Minister, Dr. Daniel F. Malan, the architect of Apartheid, that introduced us to Robert. We discussed the politics of our homeland in depth and Zelda and I were invited for dinner to the cottage in Waldorf, Maryland where he and his devoted Jewish wife, Ruth, lived about an hour away from everyone else.

I remember St. John as a tall man with a well-trimmed beard, mustache and thinning gray hair on his stately head. The tone and inflection of his voice oozed confidence when he spoke. He had an endearing smile. He attributed his longevity to gardening. He raked leaves, he planted vegetables and built a six-foot high "hedge" of leaves around his property. He liked wearing bright bow ties, all of which were made by Ruth from designer silk fabrics.

Dinner at the St. Johns' was a magnificent routine. Always a warm welcome, always ten guests, always home-cooked gourmet food and always interesting debates. After drinks in the library we were escorted to the dining room and seated in our assigned chairs. Then one of the women would be invited to unroll the wall scroll. This was the menu listing of the items to be served, each incorporating the name of a guest. This ceremony never failed to kick off an evening of fun and intellectual stimulation.

Our hosts' cottage was a little way from the main road and upon our departure around midnight, Robert would invariably take his flashlight, accompany us to our vehicle and then with his light, when the road was clear, signal us to proceed in safety on the trip back home.

When we reciprocated their kindness and had them to our home, they were usually the center of attention. Robert and Ruth always brought us something when they visited – usually a book or herbs from their own garden. From being the consummate hosts they became the consummate guests.

Ruth and Robert were loyal patrons of our store, coming to our promotions and being interested in all that we did. They would admire our jewelry and silver and were eager to learn.

I'll never forget the party at an Ambassador's home to celebrate Roberts 90th birthday.

Congratulatory messages from all corners of the globe were read to the crowd. And then it was his turn to respond. He was grateful for all the honors bestowed upon him. But what else could he possibly receive for his 100th birthday? "Start thinking," Robert suggested. We did.

And for an "early" 100th birthday at the George Washington University in Washington, D.C. he received a doctorate from Israel's Ben-Gurion University which established a chair in his name. There were letters of congratulation from Senators, Ambassadors and dignitaries from all walks of life. Such well-deserved tributes were rarely seen. This was Robert's third honorary doctorate!

What a wonderful character he was, quite unlike anyone else. We shall always remember Robert St. John, the gentile Zionist.

Secrets of a Jeweler

ROBERT ST. JOHN AND ZELDA

Izzy Heller

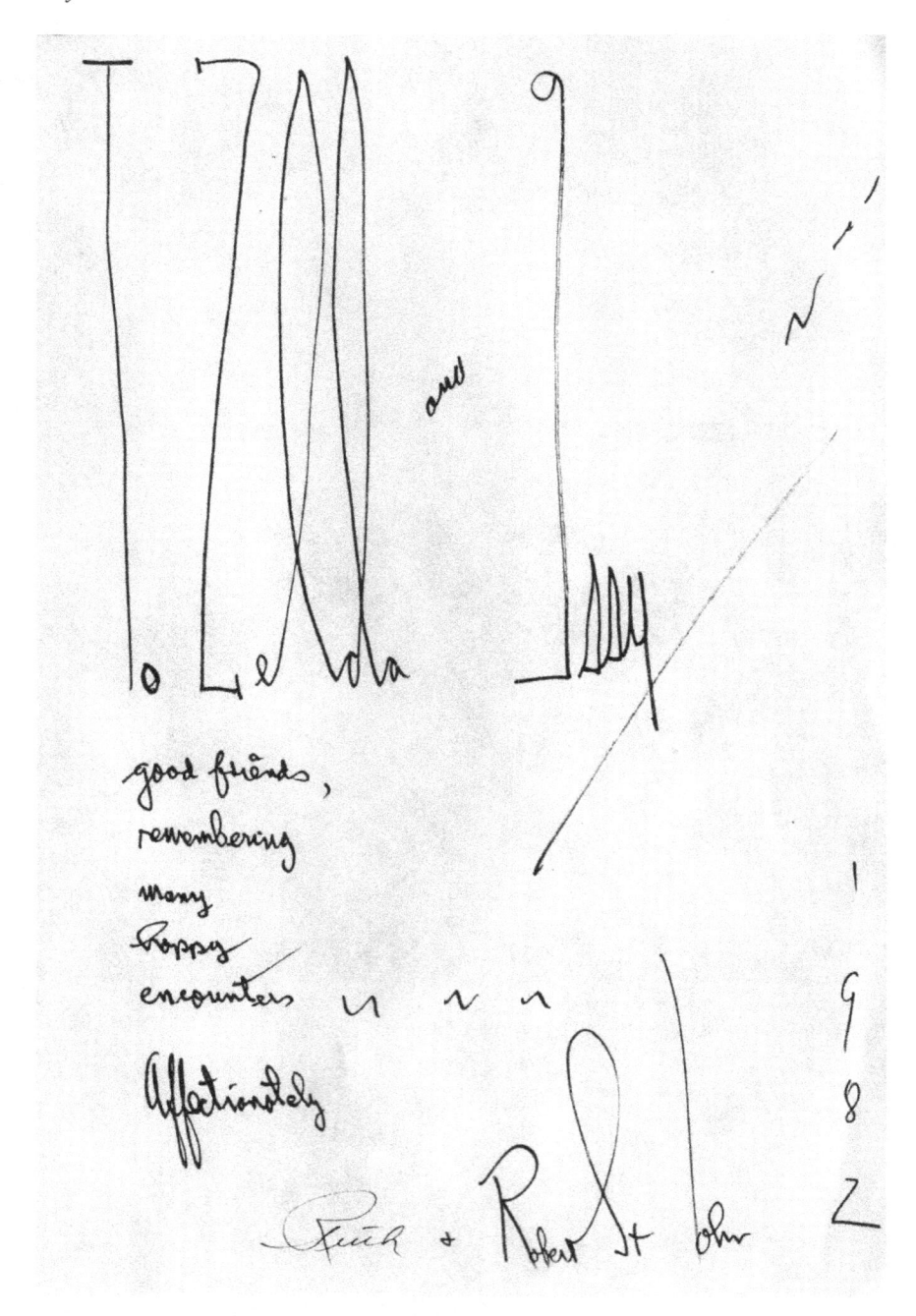

ROBERT'S MESSAGE IN THE FRONT OF HIS BOOK

THE BOYS FROM BEIRUT

I should have been an Accountant. I was so good with figures. I excelled in arithmetic, algebra and accounting. I was top of my class in mathematics. I could add and indeed often calculate, quicker than a machine.

That's why I felt so bad about my little mistake, which cost me so much.

Dor, a Lebanese Christian, was born in Beirut, a city which was widely regarded as the "Paris of the Middle East." He joined the jewelry manufacturing company owned by his father and uncle. They built up a solid business, doing work for many local jewelers.

In 1975, there was civil unrest in Lebanon and the regular army's influence was usurped by rival militias – one Christian, the other Muslim. The sound of gunfire became the norm. This conflict was to continue for many years with dire consequences. Dor's home was bombed in 1979. He rebuilt it, only to experience a repetition the next year. He, his wife and three children lived through hell. To this day, they attribute their survival to their faith.

When a large jewelry mall in downtown Beirut was looted by the Muslim faction, vaults were opened and the contents confiscated. Dor and his wife had had enough. "That's it," they said and decided to emigrate to America, where his two sisters lived.

Soon after arriving in this country in 1980, Dor joined my team as the senior bench worker, to repair and make fine jewelry. It was very different work from what he had done before. Our items were far more expensive and the work required much more care and expertise because of the delicate antique pieces which came our way. He rose to the challenge and his "golden hands" responded well. He did excellent work executing designs, sizing rings, lengthening chains, repairing watches, etc. Dor was a loyal and honest worker of mine for seven years, handling many millions of dollars of valuables. When I decided to downsize, he left us to continue on his own as an independent contractor. We have maintained our friendship.

Dor called me some time in 2003 and asked me if I was interested in buying a huge lot, approximately 25 lbs, of new gold jewelry from Lebanon. My first reaction was definitely not. Why in the world would I want to buy machine-made rings, bracelets, earrings and neckchains even if they were high karatage like 18K and 22K? Our sophisticated market in the U.S. regards this type of jewelry with apathetic interest and will pay only a small premium over metal value.

Dor thought I could buy it for the price of gold melt and suggested that I meet the owners of the gold, two brothers who were from his hometown, Beirut. He didn't know them but "friends of friends" had introduced them. He maintained they seemed motivated to sell because they needed money. What would it cost to see them? It would take only a few minutes of my time. WRONG!!!

When I saw the bags of gold the boys from Beirut brought to my office, I uttered "*oy vay.*" It was as bad as it could be. Several thousand items and 95 percent of it only good for cremation. Very little of the merchandise could be sold as jewelry.

I offered them a price per gram for the 18 karat (75 percent pure) and a higher price per gram for the 22 karat (91.7 percent pure) gold. One hundred percent pure gold is too soft to fabricate for jewelry manufacture.

After rejecting my offer, the brothers took their property and walked out, only to return a few months later to tell me they would now accept my earlier purchase prices. The international price per ounce of gold bullion had meanwhile dropped and as, I discovered later, so had the weight of their gold.

But we started again. Our manager, Nancy, spot-checked the gold contents of the various plastic bags with a touchstone and acids ("the acid test") and separated the 18 karat lot from the 22 karat lot.

We have different scales to weigh silver in troy ounces, diamonds in carats and gold in grams. Weighing gold is complicated because our scale had a maximum capacity of 400 grams, so we could not place all the 18 karat on the scale followed by the 22 karat to arrive at totals. We were obliged to weigh smaller packets one at a time. We positioned the scale so everyone could read the digital readout, which Nancy recorded on a big white desk-pad, again with visibility for all parties. As she noted each packet, the brother sitting beside her wrote the same weight in his notebook.

I have a large corner office with eight windows. While Nancy and the brothers were working at the conference table, I was at my desk near them, taking phone calls.

When the weighing was complete, the Lebanese brothers each took a pocket calculator and commenced aggregating the tabulated weights but could not agree on a total. I heard the Arabic disagreement, so I volunteered to get off the phone and enter the figures on my printing calculator. They all agreed.

There were many interruptions while I used my machine and I later learned I had placed the decimal point in an incorrect position for one of the weights. I pressed 3,675.0 instead of 367.5, a difference of 3,307.5 grams or $25,000! At the time, I read off the totals for 18 karat and 22 karat, and the one brother was quick to respond, "That's exactly what I got!"

Since we agreed on the weights I assumed them to be correct and made out the check, based on the number of grams. Yes, we overpaid them by about $25,000. They took my check and I was told, "it was a pleasure to do business with you." I'm damn sure!

In retrospect, I do not believe that the brothers came to cheat me. What happened was that the one brother saw an opportunity in my error and he grabbed it. We discovered our mistake a short while after their departure and called them to point this out. They disputed my assertion, so I stopped payment on my check and confirmed the error in a fax.

Within a few hours, I received a letter hand-delivered from their attorneys.

The gist of the letter read as follows:

> Your actions have caused my clients to suffer both emotional and financial harm. Accordingly, you are hereby advised that unless cash and/or certified funds are received by this office by close of business this Friday, we shall cause to commence to prosecute our clients rights via all available means. My clients shall take advantage

of their rights under the Maryland's Commercial Law Article, Maryland's Consumer Protection Statute, all applicable criminal statutes, as well as avail themselves of services offered by both the Montgomery County Consumer Protection Agency, The Maryland Attorney General's Office, and the media.

With these threats, I felt obliged to refer the matter to my attorney with the comment: "I won't pay these so-and-sos a dime, no matter what it costs me! I have the gold and the money, so I'm sitting pretty." My counsel was quick to point out that resolution in court would cost far more than the disputed $25,000 and could take well over a year to reach finality. Although he believed that we had the law on our side, there was no guarantee as to the outcome. At $400 per hour, my top trial lawyer did not come cheap. So I calmed down and he sent this letter to the opposition.

> I am writing in response to your letter. It is unfortunate that your clients continue to try to take advantage of Mr. Heller's mistake. It is quite apparent that your clients have not been entirely forthcoming with you about their interactions with Mr. Heller. Your claim that my client "offered to purchase gold jewelry at $xxxxx net," is in fact untrue. The parties specifically agreed that the gold would be sold by the gram, and the agreed upon price per gram was based on the "karatage" of gold. The parties agreed that the total sales price would be arrived at by an <u>accumulation</u> of weights of gold of varying karats. The correct sales price, based on the actual weight of the gold sold by your clients, was $xxxxxx.
>
> As my client's scale can weigh no more than 400 grams at a time, your clients' gold had to be weighed in a number of batches. As you have all but admitted, my client made a mistake in recording on his calculator the weight of one batch of gold, resulting in an error of approximately $25,000.00 in his computation of the sales price. It is quite clear that your clients were well aware of the mistake at the time that it was made, but, in any event, we will assume that Mr. Heller made a "unilateral mistake." Assuming

that to be the case, the general rule in Maryland as to rescission for a unilateral mistake is that

> (1) the mistake may be of such great consequences that to enforce the contract as made or offered would be unconscionable; (2) the mistake must relate to a material feature of the contract; (3) the mistake must not have come about because of the violation of a positive legal duty, or from culpable negligence; (4) the other party must be put in status quo to the extent that he suffers no serious prejudice except the loss of his bargain.

In this instance, all four conditions precedent to recision have been met. Although Mr. Heller has been fully within his rights to rescind the contract, he has in good faith offered either to return the gold to your clients, or to pay them the agreed upon price of the gold, based on its weight and karatage. Alternatively, he has graciously proposed that you and your clients meet with him to try to resolve these issues amicably. Your clients adamant insistence that a "deal is a deal," and their refusal to respond to these offers have left Mr. Heller with little choice, and consequently he rescinds the transaction.

Finally, you stated in your "Notice of Dishonored Check" that Mr. Heller is liable under 15-802 of the Md. Commercial Law Article. As you are aware, a justifiable stop payment order is a complete defense to any action brought under this section. 15-802(e)(2). For reasons we have discussed, Mr. Heller was fully justified in making the stop payment order about which you have complained. I have though, as a courtesy, enclosed a check in the amount of $35.00 as a "collection fee."

This brought a quick response from the other side and we met in the Bethesda offices of my lawyer.

After a few hours of back and forth, we reached a settlement and I made out a check. It included a premium over the contract price of some $4,000 (obviously far less than $25,000). This surcharge and my legal costs set me back somewhere in the neighborhood of a $10,000 loss.

Perhaps I should not have been an accountant.

Secrets of a Jeweler

PART OF THE GOLD ASSORTMENT FROM BEIRUT

THREE GLASS MEN

In an average year, a dozen murders are committed against jewelers in America. Scores of others in the industry are shot or injured.

Crimes cost the jewelry trade some $150 million annually.

Robbery, external theft, internal theft, burglary, Nigerian letter scams, South American gangs and fraud are some of the plagues which confront the jeweler.

Most of these crimes could be prevented with proper training and precaution.

Lee Gordon, a tough New Yorker, who ran one of the most successful diamond businesses "on the street," as the block on West 47th Street is called, believed in maximum security. His glittering palace was on the ground floor between 5th and 6th Avenues and was a long narrow store with a center passage leading all the way back to Lee's executive office, all of 120 square feet in size.

I could never sell Lee a good one-carat diamond. It was too ordinary. "Everyone on the Street has good four-grainers," (one-grain = ¼ carat). "Bring me something special," he would shout.

I did. A three-carat natural blue diamond. Lee wrote a six-figure check and thereafter treated me with some respect. He even showed me a sampling of his magnificent collection. In one safe there were thousands of G.I.A. certificates for the stones he owned, most over two carats, in all shapes and sizes.

When I needed a marquise-cut three-carater, Lee Gordon delivered. A 5-carat heart shape, he had it. Very few players had his stock. You could gaze at his shop's two windows and be dazzled in a second. He had necklaces each with a hundred carats of diamonds. He also stocked top-of-the-line rubies, emeralds and sapphires. He believed in flaunting his stunning jewelry. "Show and sell" was his motto. There would always be a group of window shoppers at Gordon's.

Lee believed in maximum security to protect his $100 million inventory: he had two armed guards in uniform on the premises. "Don't mess with Lee" was the feeling you got when you walked in to Gordon's.

Gordon's had up-to-the-minute safes with time locks and alarms. Their video surveillance system was second to none. At night, metal grids would protect the windows on the street. This was Fort Knox.

Lee Gordon did not count on the "Three Glass Men."

There so many items in his pair of windows that it took two sales assistants a good thirty minutes of hard work to unpack and display the magnificent selection each business morning. They had their work cut out for them before they could enjoy their coffee when the store opened at ten sharp.

Packing up in the evening was quicker and easier so they started at 5:30p.m. to complete the job by 5:45p.m. when the store closed. Their routine ran like clockwork.

There was a massive distraction across the road from Gordon's just before ten one morning. A big crowd had gathered at the disturbance.

At that very moment, a truck bearing the name of a New York City glass company pulled up in front of Gordon's. It had racks on both sides so glass panes could be stored vertically for protection against breakage. The "Three Glass Men" were dressed in white overalls. One was the driver, the other two his assistants. They looked the part of glass professionals.

The driver remained at the wheel with the engine running while the other men, who wore gloves and held glass clamps, ran up to the pair of windows, suction-clamped them one at a time, pulled the glass out and rested the big panes against an adjacent wall to give them ready access to the jewelry in the display showcases. They squeegeed the pieces into bags, got back into the van and took off down the narrow street.

The weeks of preparation had paid off for the criminals. The window frame fasteners had been dealt with. Their hard work, night after night, applying acid to attack the putty holding the glass windows in place had loosened the glass to the extent that their slight pulls had yielded the desired results.

The three thieves removed the multi-million dollar contents of both show windows in broad daylight! The whole operation took no more than three minutes.

The staff at Gordon's were still drinking their coffee before they realized what had happened.

The criminals were never apprehended.

Lee Gordon died a year later from cancer and the business was left to his son, Seymour, who promptly closed the shop.

PAUL THE PATRIOT

Paul is the first name of three great silversmiths whose work fetches hundreds of thousands of dollars for an item on the international market.

Paul de Lamerie (1688-1751) was born to Huguenot (Protestant) parents in Holland and came to England at age twelve. The family lived in dire poverty. He apprenticed in 1703 and ten years later was "free," the term the Guild used for graduation, to practice with his own mark in London.

The arrival of the Huguenots from France and Holland brought a style which was new to England. The impact of the new designs and methods of silversmithing was a decisive transformation in the taste for fashionable metalware.

Paul de Lamerie's work is prized for the magnificently detailed rococo decorative style. A bread basket with swing handle would incorporate cherubs, wheat sheaves, lions, flowers and garlands.

de Lamerie was the most celebrated of eighteenth-century English silversmiths. Yet his obituary in the *London Post* read: "Last Thursday died Mr. Paul de Lamerie much regretted by his Family and Acquaintance as a Tender Father, a kind Master and an upright Dealer." No mention of his brilliant skill.

Paul Storr (1771-1844) was born in London, the son of a silver-chaser (a skilled craftsman who decorates by hand). When he was fourteen, he apprenticed and gained his "freedom" in 1792 to go out on his own. Storr's early pieces show restrained taste. However, he is best known for his later work which exhibited his mastery of the grandiose neo-classical style developed in the Regency period. Massive works including vases, wine coolers, urns, centerpieces and candelabra with rococo designs bore his mark.

Paul Revere II (The Patriot) (1735-1818) was born in Boston, Massachusetts, the first son of Paul Revere I, a silversmith, from whom he learned the trade. He was nineteen when his father passed on and he carried on the family's business with his mother. Shortly thereafter the patriot embarked on the first of his military expeditions. From 1761 until 1797, excepting the period of the Revolutionary War, (1775-1778), Paul Revere II kept daybooks or ledgers. He was a master engraver, goldsmith and he advertised himself as a dentist. His silver work included pots, salvers, spoons, tankards, canns, bowls, goblets, urns, cups, baskets, and ladles. This outstanding patriot is undoubtedly the most famous silversmith in America.

In the course of conducting our business, we were fortunate to handle fine pieces by all three Pauls, but the largest and most prestigious collection we acquired was that of Paul Revere II, the Patriot.

As a child in South Africa, I had read of Revere's horse ride in the middle of the night to warn about the coming of the British troops. Little did I think I would eventually handle a collection of this hero's work, previously on exhibit at the United States Department of State, Washington, D.C.

In 1987, I purchased several magnificent items ex the collection of Mark Bortman, a collector of Revere silver who had loaned items to Mr. Clement E. Conger, in his capacity as Chairman of the Fine Arts Committee of the State Department for display in the Diplomatic Reception Rooms.

Under the Department's Project Americana, the silver on loan was shown in the rooms "where the great of the world are entertained by the Secretary of State." The Committee hoped that in time the loans would become gifts to add to the permanent collection of furnishings portraying the heritage of this country by means of the best examples available.

On the cover of the *Guidebook to the Diplomatic Reception Rooms* was the photograph of a Revere teapot. That and a sugar bowl by the same maker were the pride and joy of the silver collection.

The heirs to the Bortman estate decided to sell the collection and withdrew the loan silver from the State Department.

As I had many requests for early American silver on my want cards, I did not hesitate in buying the teapot, sugar bowl and several other pieces when they were offered to me. Those purchases appeared to be very expensive at the time. Today they are so "affordable."

It was great fun to research some of the items, as I did for a punch ladle. By referring to the meticulous records in the day books housed in the Boston Museum of Fine Arts, we traced the exact weight, the date it was finished, for whom it was made and the price charged.

I sold most of the collection almost immediately to one collector who had been persistent in his quest for Revere silver. He was thrilled to gain several pieces in one swoop.

However, three months later he had "buyer's remorse" and thought he had been impulsive and possibly overpaid. I offered to refund his money. He would think about it, he said.

My customer never returned the silver. Years later, he sold it at a public auction in New York which I attended. Before the sale, there was much hype put out in public relations announcements about American history and the national heritage in regard to the Revere silver. It worked. I sat quietly in amazement when the prices realized ten times my client's cost. Hindsight is akin to 20/20 vision.

Izzy Heller

A PAUL REVERE TEAPOT

NANCY PEERY

A new customer introduced herself. Nancy Peery was pretty, blonde and vivacious. Within minutes of my introduction, it became obvious she did everything at double-speed. She outpaced everyone with her walking and speaking.

Her request was simple. She wanted a large silver-plated punchbowl. We had just the thing and I quoted her the ticket price. She asked if that was the best price. I assured her it was and she accepted my reply and made her first purchase.

Over the years, Nancy Peery became a loyal client and we got to know and befriend both her and her husband, Dick. The two met in 1961 at The University of Utah, and on their first date went dancing. Now Dick is Nancy's "P.R.officer" and photographer at her singing recitals. He would be gentlemanly, friendly and humble and only later did I learn that he was the co-owner of Hot Shoppes, which was our neighboring tenant in the Barlow Building. That restaurant served tasty home-cooked meals at very affordable prices. I enjoyed their 75 cent luncheon blue plate (12" diameter) specials. My favorite was a vegetarian selection of macaroni and cheese, succotash, and carrots. When we took overseas visitors to a meal next door at Hot Shoppes, they could not believe the value.

Hot Shoppes, like the other subsidiaries in Dick's conglomerate, was known as one of the best employers around. Zelda and I decided this was a company we could invest in and bought stock. We have done very well and still hold the shares today.

On August 29, 2002, Dick was invited to address a class of graduating students at Brigham Young University in Utah. I have a transcript of that speech which is quite remarkable for its good common sense. He told of his father's reply to the frequently asked question "What is the secret to your success?" The response was that three elements were integral: being born right, developing good habits and marrying right. With this came caveats: success is never final, for change is constant; watch the details; expect perfection; lead a balanced life; be active in your community. In my contacts with Dick and Nancy, it is obvious that they adhere to this philosophy.

Meanwhile, as the business of Heller Jewelers grew, we needed more space and we expanded to the side and back of our premises. It was difficult to have builders "within our walls" and keep the show running. Customer service and security were compromised.

One day as a construction laborer was hammering away at old drywall, Nancy walked in. She could see I was flustered at the noise and debris on the one hand and the needs of the clientele on the other. So what did she do? She removed her jacket, took off her shoes and commenced picking up chunks of board and taking them to the dumpster. At first I protested and said it was not necessary. But she said it was her duty and pleasure to help us. By the time she was through, her hair and clothes were very dusty and dirty. Throughout, she was cheerful and chatty. She was an absolute joy.

We were invited to a Gilbert and Sullivan performance where Nancy was the star performer. Later, we attended her recitals at different venues and her strong and confident soprano voice never failed to stun the audience. This was virtuoso stuff. I learned that she had performed in numerous theatres including the Kennedy Center in Washington, D.C., with the Morman Tabernacle Choir in Salt Lake City, Utah, and abroad in Austria and Israel.

In addition to her dedication to her home and her family, Nancy Peery was devoted to church and community activities. She taught Sunday School classes to the teenagers in the Church of Jesus Christ of Latter-day Saints, organized charity events, and she gave generously of her time and money to worthwhile causes.

Although serious about her priorities, she is a fun person to be with. She brings smiles to those around her. At American Red Cross Galas, which she has chaired twelve times, she sings the National Anthem passionately and beautifully. At one such an event, Nancy referred me to the items being auctioned. The very last was the free use of a beachfront mansion (eight bedrooms, six bathrooms) in Nags Head, North Carolina for ten days. I found that when bidding took place my hand was going up and up. After all, it would be nice to have the family together on vacation. Zelda looked at me as though I was crazy when I bid $2,500.00. "What if the house turns out to be rat-infested?" she wanted to know. Before I could reassure her, my dinner companion exclaimed: "It's not rat- infested! I should know: it's my home." That taken care of, we bought the "time share" for $3,000.00 and had the best holiday ever.

At a recent Red Cross charity event, the theme of Nancy's choosing was "Put Your Shoulder to the Wheel." She motivated everyone with her energy and devotion and a record amount was raised for this wonderful charity.

Each December, we receive a colorful family photograph from Nancy and Dick together with an invitation to attend a seasonal festive open house party. We always enjoy going to their magnificent home which Nancy and Dick decorate traditionally. The bright and colorful lights in the garden and the thousands of trinkets indoors make these visits memorable. No staff is in evidence, family and friends assist. We always look forward to seeing the fruit punch served from "our" bowl, the one which brought us together.

When Dick's mother, the matriarch of the family, passed on, I was called to do a valuation of the silver and jewelry and Zelda was asked to sell the house. We worked hard on these missions and soon thereafter got a referral to do an enormous house-and-contents sale for their elderly aunt and uncle who were leaving Maryland. That estate sale was so large it took all of six days to close.

And now I need to tell you about an event which cemented our relationship with Dick and Nancy.

Long ago in distant South Africa, Zelda produced a great variety concert for charity. She dreamed about repeating that endeavor in the States. So in the year 2002, Zelda decided to produce a musical theater concert in Rockville, Maryland, to raise funds for a very worthwhile cause, the Children's Inn at the National Institutes of Health.

The Children's Inn is a private, non-profit charitable organization dependent on contributions for its daily operational needs. Each year it provides safe and caring accommodations for over one thousand children and their families who call the Inn home. These children, generally with rare and life-threatening diseases, receive therapies at the adjoining hospital, which is the top research facility in the world.

The idea of the concert was for gifted children to perform to aid sick children and so "KIDS FOR KIDS!" was born.

Zelda placed advertisements in the *Washington Post* in search of child performers. The talent hunt brought an immediate response, and for many evenings we were auditioning applicants, a few of whom were outstanding. One had played at Carnegie Hall, others were destined for Broadway. The hardest part of the exercise was saying to those unsuccessful: "Don't call us. We'll call you." In fact, we called everyone, whether yes or no.

With the help of Richard Hartzell of The Musical Theater Center, one hundred performers sang, danced and played in two concerts which took place over Memorial Day weekend. They were very successful. We were exhausted.

Everyone in our family pitched in to assist in various capacities. As C.E.O., Zelda needed all the help she could get. I produced the booklet with messages, program, bios of performers, thank yous and of course ADVERTISEMENTS. I sent out over one thousand video tapes with solicitations appealing to the affluent of the metro area to donate.

Our daughter Tania and her family were backstage, helping with the props and costumes.

During the intermission, my job was to sell snacks and drinks for $1 each. Nancy and Dick attended one of the concerts and were very encouraging. Dick paid me $1 for a candy bar.

Their monetary support went well beyond that candy bar. The following week we received $50,000 from the Marriotts to our cause. The total net proceeds just exceeded $100,000 and Nancy and Dick had given half!

Nancy does not sit idly for a minute: she's always working. She once showed me her schedule for the week: meetings, practice sessions, classes, travel – she's one busy gal.

Nancy is no pushover. I was with her during a telephone conversation she had with a delinquent landscape contractor, who was giving excuse after excuse for his tardiness. She kept her cool and it became obvious he understood her very well when she firmly stated, "that's your problem!" Nancy Peery is a delightful woman who has her own identity and enjoys life to the full as Nancy Peery Marriott. Dick is of course, Richard E. Marriott, Chairman of the Board of Host Marriott Corporation.

Secrets of a Jeweler

RICHARD MARRIOTT, NANCY PEERY MARRIOTT, ZELDA AND IZZY

A LADY AND HER HAMMERS

I wish I could say that I discovered her. In fact she found me. She came to me for a silver appraisal of an object she had made. Little did I realize when I saw the tiny, middle-aged, bespectacled lady that she would turn out to be a premier silversmith – Washington's own Georg Jensen (the Danish master craftsman 1866-1935) That was apparent to me the moment the pair of candlesticks were taken out of the wrapping towels.

Dorothy K. Gordon was born in Boston, Massachusetts in May 1919. Ever since early childhood she loved to do creative things – painting, sewing, embroidering or metal work. She attended Boston public schools, and won a scholarship in her senior year in an art competition. After graduating from art school, she had difficulty in finding work in the field of art and so took positions in the world of business and government during the depression years. She managed to continue painting in her limited free time during these and subsequent years, even with the rearing of three children. When the last of the brood finally left home, several hours of leisure time daily became hers to devote to her beloved field of art.

A friend of Dorothy took her to a pottery class. She tried her hand at throwing pots, but it was not her thing. The clay was slimy and squishy and made her cringe. So she tried Japanese wood block printing. Again, she found this experience unsatisfactory. She happened to go to a "Creative Crafts" show held at the Smithsonian Institution and saw hand-made jewelry and other metalwork and knew instantly this was her forte.

She felt she needed and was determined to get instruction. When she saw an ad in the newspaper announcing the YWCA was going to hold classes in jewelry making, she enrolled immediately.

Dorothy Gordon says in her autobiography: "I loved metal and it loved me, and it has been a most successful and happy marriage ever since. After doing just jewelry for a couple of years, I wanted to know more about metals. Catholic University of America held classes in hollowware, attended mostly by seminarians and nuns. I applied and was accepted and took the class for two summer semesters. My teacher, Rufus Jacoby, and an excellent one at that, told me I had learned all he had to teach me and suggested that I go out on my own. So I did.

I have been happily working by myself since then and making what, I hope, have been beautiful pieces. In 1985, I took a course at Montgomery College, Maryland with Fred Fenster, of the University of Wisconsin, who further inspired me.

Most of my hollowware work has been made for people I love – my children and grandchildren and for my own home use."

A very small number of Dorothy's pieces were sold at craft shops. Because everything that bore her stamp *DEVORAH* (her Hebrew name) was made solely by her without any help, her output was very limited.

It is rare for an item of silver to be made entirely by the same hand, even if the craftsman is proficient in all aspects of the trade. Normally skilled specialists would be used for such work as engraving, casting, embossing, gilding or stone setting.

Several times, I asked her to make me an object, but she was always too busy – usually making ceremonial art objects for her family or the Washington Hebrew Congregation where several pieces of hers are on display in their permanent Judaica Collection.

The basic tool of the silversmith is a hammer. Dorothy labors daily on her own, beating hard at the thick metal, shaping it to her liking with thousands of blows. Alas, the noise of the hammers has caused her hearing to become impaired. I once felt her biceps. She smiled because she knew her muscular arms were impressive. At the back of her home in Northwest Washington, her well- equipped workshop has been the birthplace of some of the finest silverware ever crafted in this region.

Even with her great talent, she could not have achieved what she did without the loving support of her husband, Benjamin. They are inseparable.

Dorothy K. Gordon was featured in a Home and Garden Television Network program series *Modern Masters* in 2003.

She has exhibited at the Smithsonian Institution, churches, synagogues, the Boston Society of Arts and Crafts, museums and also at the home of Zelda and Izzy Heller in Bethesda, Maryland.

In 1994, we hosted a meeting of the American Silver Guild and I arranged for Dorothy to explain and demonstrate the design and creation of a completely handmade piece of sterling hollowware. Members of the A.S.G. were captivated by her straightforward and charming address and were awestruck at her accomplishments in artistic silverware.

At the age of 85, she is still an active metalsmith and hopes to continue for some time to come. She still does everything by hand, "as was done in the days of Theophilus, and I will keep doing so – too old to change! Every piece is made with love – love for the sheer joy of creating a thing of beauty, and for the person who is going to receive it."

I have had the pleasure of appraising much of Dorothy's work. I like to think I encouraged her in the hard search for creative beauty. After all it's not every day that in one's own backyard, one has a Georg Jensen.

Secrets of a Jeweler

DOROTHY K. GORDON MASTER JEWELER AND SILVERSMITH

Izzy Heller

A DOROTHY GORDON MASTERPIECE

THE KING OF BANKRUPTCY

The chairman of a large Washington bank once referred to the attorney as "The King of Bankruptcy" for his dominance in this specialist field of the law.

Henry E. Beck was a small man who had a brilliant mind. In his day he negotiated many large insolvencies with banks, other creditors, courts and stockholders. At the end of discussions in a case, all parties were not so unhappy that they could not follow Henry's recommendations.

A dapper dresser, Henry always sported a stickpin in his tie. In fact, he had probably a hundred pins to choose from.

Some businessmen were scared to be seen having lunch with him in fear of the interpretation by onlookers as an indication of financial difficulty.

With his head for legal analysis came an eye for art. Beck invested his disposable income in contemporary paintings by relatively unknown artists. His collection did not meet the criteria for "popular taste." Most of the public would probably regard the works as bizarre, macabre or even grotesque. The experts would call them surrealistic.

Caribbean, South American, French, Baltimore artists were among those represented in his purchases which cluttered the walls, closets and basement of his home near Rock Creek Park in Washington, D.C.

Mr. and Mrs. Henry Beck were very loving and they were excellent ballroom dancers. At charity events, the handsome and talented couple were always featured on the dance floor. Their happy marriage of 45 years came to an end with her passing.

The usually confident Henry could not cope with his loss. Gradually he disengaged from his legal practice. He had difficulty in managing his personal affairs. Initially he could not bring himself to part with his home, but he commenced to "thin out" his copious acquisitions. His only child, best described as a hippie, had no interest whatsoever in "possessions."

That brought Henry to me and I purchased his late wife's magnificent jewelry. We also cataloged hundreds of prints, paintings, sculptures, decorative accessories and furniture. By the time all this was done, we had become good friends.

Over the next few years, Henry donated major works of art, most of which had appreciated substantially, to museums and galleries. One large painting which was a charitable contribution was by the famous Bolero.

Henry then decided to volunteer his time at a local hospital as an orderly to patients being admitted. The once-famous lawyer wearing a red jacket, was proud of his new job, wheeling the sick around Sibley Hospital.

As he aged, he showed signs of senility and could no longer continue with his home. Zelda as a top realtor with Long & Foster, was given the listing and she obtained a good price for the house despite its poor state of repair, mainly because of its great location. With the onset of Alzheimers, "The King of Bankruptcy" is now a resident in a nursing home. There, in his apartment, hangs some of his favorite art from floor to ceiling. He still likes chocolates, but no longer knows me or even his son.

MY BANKERS, GOD BLESS THEM!

When I emigrated in 1980, I left behind an unbroken association of sixty years which my Dad and his sons had with our bankers, The Standard Bank of South Africa.

To have such a lengthy relationship with a bank was not unusual there. With only five banks, all very large, clients loyally stuck with their choice. You knew the people at the bank and they knew you. It was like a marriage.

What a contrast in the States. A different bank at every corner. Competition was good. My business was sought after. I was advised by my C.P.A. to incur debt to establish a good credit record! This appeared to be a contradiction of what I was taught. I was also advised not to deal with only one bank because it was safer to split one's business.

Over the next two decades "the urge to merge" amongst Washington banks was such my bank of choice had three different names in three years. New faces appeared monthly. I became an unknown. I resorted to toll-free telephone numbers to get information. I had to yield to finger-printing to cash my own check at my own branch. None of these developments pleased me. It was unsettling.

One Monday morning, I received a message from my bank manager, whom I had never met, to advise my business account was substantially overdrawn. I knew that was unlikely because at the time we had a policy of keeping a minimum balance of $50,000. I said I would look into it. I rushed to my bookkeeper, Sue, who confirmed what I knew. She showed me her documentation which indicated a healthy balance of some $70,000.

Sue and I walked to the bank with our records and reconciled all debits. However, there were no deposits entered in the bank's books for a week. We produced our deposit slips with the bank's confirmation stamp. How could it be we were not credited?

And then Sue spotted it. The printed deposit slips which the bank had given us for our account had the name and account number of another client, a church. A batch of that client's forms had been interspersed with ours. Over $100,000.00 had been placed in the wrong account. We could relax. The error was immediately corrected, but no apology was ever offered.

With the rush to consolidate and save costs, the merging banks often did not plan sufficiently so there was confusion, multiple errors, low staff morale and customer dissatisfaction.

I discovered a bank error in my favor of over $200,000.00 and reported it immediately. I was brushed aside with "it cannot be." Only my persistence over a two-month period rectified the entry. Again, no one said "sorry." Certainly not "thank you."

The head office of the bank was moved to North Carolina and a woman from Charlotte was put in charge of the sizable loan department locally. Her secretary summoned me to an important meeting in the bank's downtown D.C. office.

The pretty girl with the southern drawl did not mince words with me. Her new management team viewed "relationship banking" as a thing of the past and had taken a strategic decision that they no longer wanted the business of jewelers. Accordingly my line of credit for $600,000.00 was being terminated immediately.

I was in shock. We had never been late for an obligation. We were liquid and profitable. They had adequate collateral. What was the reason for this new policy?

Fortunately I had the resources to pay down the balance of my loan. Unfortunately there were other jewelers who could not.

The final straw of my frustration was the forged check in 1998.

It was my habit to scan through copies of our paid checks each month when our statement arrived. I spotted one check bearing my signature which was smaller than the others. It was for $9,250.00 and was handwritten. I did not recognize the writing. It had our Heller logo, our name and address. But it had no telephone number like our other checks. The payee was unknown to me and the memo section was unclear. This was very fishy. How was it that it bore my signature?

I telephoned my bank and after being shunted from one person to the next, eventually got through to the "specialist" who dealt with fraud. She said she would get the original check from the archives within a week and then I should come to her office and if confirmed as a fake, I was to complete an affidavit to that effect. The check was duly produced and I marveled at the reproduction of the paper, our logo and especially my signature!

I asked for a prompt reversal of the charge to my account, but I was told by the "specialist" that she did not have the authority to accede.

In the course of the following two months, my branch manager first declined my request, which decision I said was unacceptable, then offered to settle the matter with an ex gratia allowance of $4,625.00 (50 percent) and finally, when I said I was taking my business elsewhere, he agreed to a full credit. What a battle! I never learned whether the bank was insured against the risk.

The person responsible for the fraud was charged and I was subpoenaed to appear in Silver Spring Court as a witness for the prosecution. The bank was also asked to give evidence in the case. I waited at the courthouse for several hours for the bank's representative to appear. After a reminder phone call from the clerk of the court, we learned the bank was too busy to press charges. The case was dismissed.

The loyalty to my bank, which I had brought with me from South Africa, had dissipated. I decided to take my business elsewhere.

I listed what I wanted from my next bank and they included the following:

- sound financials (since I loaned them money from time to time)
- size to be small enough to give me personal attention and yet sufficiently large to offer a wide range of services
- proximity to my store, with a drive-by window

The National Capital Bank (N.C.B.) met my three requirements and I opened an account there. It was one of my best business decisions.

The bank was established in 1889 and its financial ratios are of the best in the country. For several generations the Didden family has run this bank in a personal, conservative fashion. George A. Didden III is Chairman of the Board of Directors and his three brothers, Richard, Donald and James serve with him. Its staff is so loyal there is hardly a turnover. Service is paramount to N.C.B.

The bank opened a branch in Chevy Chase and wanted to publicize this new entity. Their advertising agent approached me for an endorsement which I gladly agreed to then and there. These were my sincere words which she tape-recorded as I spoke:

> "I've been in business for more than forty-five years, both here and abroad – and banking with NCB reminds me of the good old days. NCB is a family business, managed by the four brothers Didden. I am one of four sons, and can relate to and admire them. I am all for relationship banking. We know the personalities at the bank, and they know us. Nothing is too much trouble for them. For example, when I order a foreign exchange draft to pay for imports, they offer to deliver it to my store.
>
> Where else in 1999 do you find service like this? I believe that, with mergers and takeovers, clients can sense the tension and insecurity of the staff at bigger banks. I have been there. Everything gets referred to someone else. I do not like dealing with the nameless and the faceless. I admire the security and sincerity of a family business established more than one hundred years ago. NCB has taken the trouble to get to know our operation, and are therefore interested and knowledgeable bankers. Quick decisions are their forte. I enjoy dealing with NCB. I heartily recommend them as your banker."

George Didden has served as a Regional Director of the Federal Reserve Board and is on the National Board of the Smithsonian Institution. He and his wife, Kathy are close friends and to our delight have become our neighbors.

Secrets of a Jeweler

In 2003 Zelda was invited to join the Board of the Bank. When she accepted, she became the first woman director in the long history of N.C.B. Today she serves too on its Executive Committee. Her expertise in real estate matters is her contribution.

N.C.B. has resisted merging or being taken over. Its stock is traded very thinly "over the counter." Very few holders sell. They are in for the long haul. They have confidence in the bank, as I do.

The loyalty to my bank has been restored.

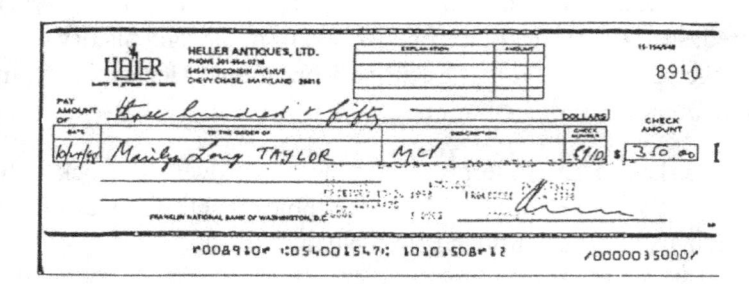

Check: 8910   Amt: $350.00   Date: 10/27/98

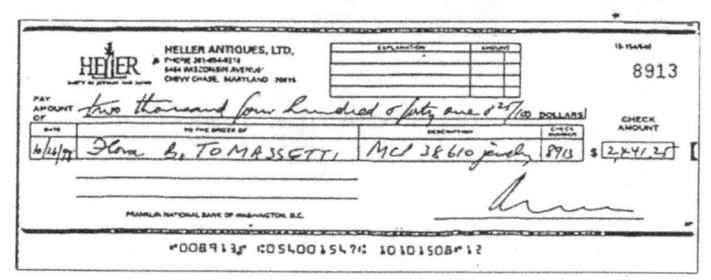

Check: 8913   Amt: $2,441.25 Date: 10/28/98

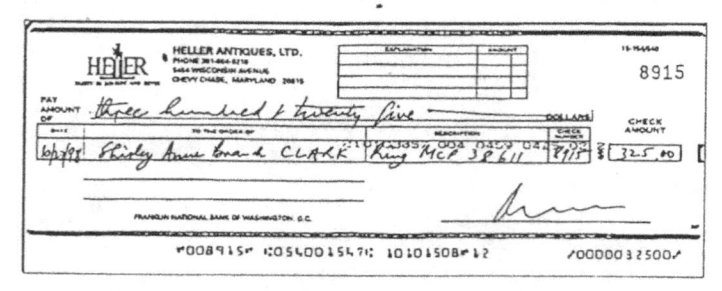

Check: 8915   Amt: $325.00   Date: 10/28/98

Check: 8971   Amt: $9,250.00 Date: 10/21/98

CAN YOU PICK OUT THE FRAUDULENT CHECK?

Secrets of a Jeweler

THE DIDDEN BROTHERS OF NATIONAL CAPITAL BANK

"Where else do you find service like this today?"

> I've been in business for more than 45 years, both here and abroad – and banking with NCB reminds me of the good old days. NCB is a family business, managed by the four brothers Didden. I am one of four sons, and can relate to and admire them. I am all for relationship banking. We know the personalities at the bank, and they know us. Nothing is too much trouble for them. For example, when I order a foreign exchange draft to pay for imports, they offer to deliver it to my store.
>
> Where else in 1999 do you find service like this? I believe that, with mergers and takeovers, clients can sense the tension and insecurity of the staff at bigger banks. I have been there. Everything gets referred to someone else. I do not like dealing with the nameless and the faceless. I admire the security and sincerity of a family business established more than 100 years ago. NCB has taken the trouble to get to know our operation, and are therefore interested and knowledgeable bankers. Quick decisions are their forte. I enjoy dealing with NCB. I heartily recommend them as your banker.

Izzy Heller, owner, Heller Jewelers of Chevy Chase

We'd like to thank Mr. Heller for being our customer. If you'd like to get this kind of service for yourself, just give us a call. We are here to help. **Washington's hometown bank.**

THE NATIONAL CAPITAL BANK
OF WASHINGTON

5228 44th Street, N.W. • (202) 966-2688
316 Pennsylvania Ave., S.E. • (202) 546-8000

Member FDIC

IZZY ENDORSING THE BANK

MY DANCING PARTNER

One of the perks of my jewelry career has been the friendship with a man bearing the unusual name of Fishel Beigel, a.k.a. "The Fish."

Fishel was born in Brooklyn, New York in 1956 and is twenty-two years my junior. Today his full beard gives him the appearance of being my contemporary. Fishel is an orthodox Jew whose parents came from Poland. He is a colorful personality, but as a Chasid, he wears the typical heavy black garb of his group.

He was first schooled at the Bobover Yeshiva in Brooklyn and later, for two years, at Stamfod Hill, London, England.

When he was twenty, he became a diamond broker in Manhattan acting as a liaison between sellers and buyers for a small commission, representing many of the world's largest diamond cutters. This he did for almost ten years.

In 1985, Fishel teamed up with a business acquaintance of long standing, Rick Shatz. Rick has a very different background to that of his partner and was not brought up in the orthodox tradition of Jewry. He obtained a Bachelor of Science degree in Aerospace Engineering, which may have helped in his dealing with the technical aspects of cutting and grading of diamonds. Rick is very "into" golf, a sport which is anathema to The Fish.

Since his association with Fishel, Rick has become more observant and wears a *KIPPAH* (skullcap). He draws the line at growing a beard and has remained clean-shaven.

The partnership created a unique pair that could rival the famous show, "The Odd Couple." Different as they are, the individuals share professionalism, integrity and a great sense of humor.

Together Rick and Fishel have built a thriving enterprise in diamonds. They are now one of the largest players in diamonds in New York City. Their special spheres of influence are with old mine estate diamonds, diamond jewelry and natural yellow diamonds. Perhaps because the partners are so dissimilar, they respect each other and get on so well. Fishel is somewhat emotional and has highs and lows. Rick is more even in nature. It is said that one needs both an accelerator and a brake for a vehicle to perform efficiently.

I first met The Fish on a cold call 18 years ago when he and Rick shared, with a family member, a smoke-laden tiny office in the Diamond District of Manhattan. He bought several diamonds from me and I took his check without question. He wanted to know why I trusted him with such a large sum. He challenged me: how did I know his paper was good? I responded: "No con-artist would ever choose the name of Fishel Beigel." We have been good friends since that day and have done some sizable business together.

On a subsequent visit, I discussed a namesake, Rabbi Heller. Yomtov Lipman Heller lived in Prague many centuries before and was a prominent scholar and commentator on scripture. I had an English translation of his biography with me detailing his arrest on trumped-up charges and his subsequent vindication. Thereafter Fishel and Rick have referred to me as "Reb Izzy," an unearned title I revere.

Fishel Beigel is a remarkable person for many reasons. He has great charisma and people gather round him. He is honest and hard-working. He loves to buy and sell. He is highly intelligent and constantly barrages one with questions to enhance his vast knowledge. He is interested in everyone and everything. He has traveled extensively to Brazil, Belgium, India, Israel, Hong Kong, Switzerland and Thailand, which is unusual for one in his religious group which has a tendency to the insular.

In the years from 1983 to 2000, Fishel acted in a volunteer position as an emergency medical technician being on call as a driver of an ambulance. He has saved the lives of many people and has helped in the delivery of six babies.

Fishel is gifted with a magnificent singing tenor voice. He has produced two albums of Yiddish Classics. He is often called upon to be a *BAAL-TEFILA* (the lead cantor of prayer) at services.

Like all orthodox Jews, devout observance is priority and business activity comes to an abrupt halt at certain times for prayer. Groups gather in various select offices, including those of Rick Shatz, Inc. at about 4p.m.

daily for afternoon (*MINCHA*) recitals. After fifteen minutes, the crowd disperses and individuals revert to their respective secular lives.

For all his charm, Fishel is no pushover. He can *HUNDEL* (negotiate) like the best of them. To support his position, he may draw on Talmudic scholarship quoting letter and verse. He is a hard bargainer and dislikes losing. Having said that, one of the reasons I was drawn to him was he believes in a win-win outcome, in particular "something should be left on the table for the other party."

In his office, there is food and drink for everyone who visits. This is quite a commitment because the offices of Rick Shatz, Inc. are constantly busy, quite like a miniature Grand Central Station.

A central tenet of Jewish belief is the sanctity of life, the here and the now. The number "18" represents *CHAI* or life. So Fishel occupies the 18th floor of his building and incorporates 18 in his telephone number.

Fishel's wife, Esther or Esty, is the child of a father from Poland and a mother from Czechoslovakia. Fishel and Esty make a great team and are blessed with five children and nine grandchildren.

One year in Miami Beach, Florida, we had quite a philosophical inter-family discussion over dinner in a kosher Chinese restaurant. The Beigel family were represented by Fishel, Esty and their eighteen year-old daughter. We, the Heller's, consisted of Zelda, me, and our daughter Tania. The company was good and the wide-ranging dialogue likewise.

We discussed Zelda's occupation of realtor and Fishel indicated the selling of fixed property was a career he had considered. But he had ruled it out. "Why?" we asked. His answer saddened me. "Can you imagine an agent dressed like me?"

We also raised the question of arranged marriages – with or without a *SHADCHEN* (marriage broker) - which was the norm in the Chassidic community. How could a bride or a groom have a partner chosen by outsiders? The three-prong answer was as follows. Firstly, the choice is made by insiders who know the congregation and who know the natures of the young people. Secondly, the decision is not made by the elders, whose role is to present suitable candidates for consideration. Either party can reject a suitor. And thirdly, 50 percent of all marriages in the U.S. end in

Secrets of a Jeweler

divorce whereas in the orthodox sector, the percentage in minimal. The Beigel teen-age daughter nodded in agreement. A year later, we were at her wedding, the result of an arrangement by the parents of the bridal couple.

Zelda and I were privileged to have been invited to the lavish weddings of two of the Beigel children. Chassidic weddings are loud, happy celebrations. They are also segregated affairs. Men and women are seated separately. They also dance separately. On each occasion I was part of a large circle of men, and shuffled to the beat of loud music. When invited, I danced with Fishel, the father of the bride. Likewise Zelda was given an honor of a dance with Esty, the mother of the bride, behind the division on the other side of the hall. After the marriage ceremony, a wonderful dinner was served at which time certain men made their appearance to collect charitable contributions to various causes. By their activity, you are given the opportunity of doing a *MITZVAH* (good deed) to help the sick, the needy or other worthy causes. There is no prohibition of alcohol at a Chassidic wedding. In fact, liquor flows in abundance at the tables. Everyone is very joyous and "the voices of the bride and groom are heard everywhere."

At community ceremonies, the Chassidic men display beautiful tailoring. The design of Fishel's big fur hat, which he wears on holidays and special occasions, originates from the nobility of Russia and Poland some two hundred years ago.

In the directors' corner office of Rick Shatz, Inc., on the wall near Fishel's L-shaped desk, hangs a picture of a Jewish hero, Rabbi Shlomo Halberstam (1907-2000), known lovingly as "the Rebbe."

The leader of the Bobover movement of Chassidic Judaism for over five decades, Rabbi Halberstam was ranked as one of the world's foremost religious scholars and from his Brooklyn neighborhood, exerted an influence which was felt worldwide. While his large white beard may have made his appearance old-fashioned, he was well versed in today's world and reached out with enthusiasm to all people in his pursuit of compassion, virtue and education. Other leaders turned to him for advice. Each day he would personally receive many visitors who poured out their hearts to him and looked for solace and advice. He stressed to each that even small acts of kindness could impact the world beneficially. He was known to discern even a small ray of hope from any problem.

It has always been obvious to me that Fishel, in his way of life, is devoted to the ideals of the man who looks down on him, Rabbi Halberstam.

There are those critics who say the orthodox Jews are extremists who have no room in their equation for others. But for me, in a world beset by the questions of who we are and where we are going, it is uplifting to associate with a person like Fishel Beigel, my dancing partner, who is well-anchored and who believes fervently in life, justice, charity, good deeds and *SHALOM* (Peace).

Secrets of a Jeweler

FISHEL BEIGEL AND IZZY

ETHICS IN THE JEWELRY TRADE

The campus of Indiana University at Bloomington is a delight. Set amidst beautiful trees, it is so much nicer than the harsh big-city nature of a school like George Washington University in downtown D.C.

I was a resident student at Bloomington for a short time while taking courses for an appraisal qualification. I have been a member of the International Society of Appraisers (I.S.A.) for many years and as part of a continuing education program have lectured on several topics. One such topic was ETHICS.

The talk was at a meeting of the National Capital Area's chapter of the I.S.A. and was well attended and, based on the questions and discussions at the end of my remarks, was a subject of considerable interest.

Both the I.S.A. and the J.A. (Jewelers of America) have codes of ethics, which these organizations regard as fundamental to gain the confidence of the public in the honesty, integrity and professionalism of their members.

ETHICS is defined as the obligation of moral duty to achieve the highest good. This is different from LEGALITY and much more difficult to practice. However, the obligation is real and must be addressed on all fronts. Sometimes what constitutes ethical behavior is not clear-cut.

Both the above mentioned codes of ethics list the requirements to include:

- maintenance of a high level of personal and professional integrity
- continuing education in our profession
- promoting activities for the good of the community
- rendering service based on truth and honor
- treating customers as we would like to be treated
- honest representation of the product or service offered

- refraining from belittling a competitor with disparaging statements

- confidentiality of a relationship with a client

Now, with the myriad of conscious and subconscious decisions we managers have to make on a daily basis, how many of them fall short of these noble ethical standards? Ah, the dilemmas of conscience. For myself, I know the bar is set much higher now than it was earlier in my career. In fact, I wish I could reverse and correct conduct that I now view as ethically unbecoming.

Why should a jeweler be concerned about Ethics? For several very good reasons in order to set a guideline for others to follow.

Our conduct, our example, has a direct impact on our staff and our suppliers. (Did we refrain from buying diamonds from conflict areas for ethical reasons BEFORE this trade became illegal? Did we refrain from not disclosing laser treatment of diamonds BEFORE this conduct became illegal? Have we ever sold radio-active blue Topaz?)

Advertising can be honest or dishonest. The way we promote has an effect on our community. Do we want the public to become cynical and not willing to trust our trade because we advertise "right-out-of-the-mines;" "don't buy retail" (when sales tax is charged and therefore by definition, the sale is retail): less 60 percent off (off what?) and so on.

Pricing policy also demands ethical restraint. When gold rose dramatically in 1980 to $800 an ounce, jewelers' inventories were re-ticketed upwards, but when gold dropped how long did it take to put new lower price tags on the merchandise? Likewise when the price of silver dropped from $50 to $6 per ounce (who said metals were a good, safe investment?) and many stores maintained prices for a year thereafter.

We frown on the "F" word, the "N" word and the "D" word, the latter for Discrimination. I challenged my audience by asking them if they discriminated against customers, remember, not legally but ethically, when they accepted an American Express card from one client and cash from another. In the case of the card, the net payment could be only 96 percent of the price. Should the second client not receive a 4 percent discount to achieve parity? Are we not discriminating against the better customer?

Many of us try to re-activate dormant accounts by bribing them with a $10 store credit on their next purchase. How do our loyal active clients feel when they are excluded from recognition?

Confidentiality is listed as an ethical obligation and yet our industry has disregarded the right to privacy by selling the names of customers @ $80 per thousand, not once, but over and over.

Most shopping for jewelry is done by women, yet the boards of directors of most corporations in the industry consist predominately of men.

Do the salespeople tell clients that most gemstones are "treated"? Do they print this on their invoices? Those salespeople are sure to shout when their gemstones are "untreated" and command a price premium.

Are you a jeweler who will puff an appraisal to appease a client because "the insurance company can afford it?"

The question of what constitutes right and wrong is troubling, but it must be addressed, not avoided. The moral leadership must come from the top in a business and indeed in the nation.

There exists a total lack of restraint on the part of many top public figures who advance themselves rather than the general interest. This says something disturbing about the national character. Betrayal and greed are unsettling our standards.

Is the golden rule now that GOLD RULES?

What do these names have in common? Spiro Agnew, Oliver North, Robert McFarland, Marion Barry, Michael Deaver, Ivan Boesky, Gary Hart, Clayton Lonetree, Jim and Tammy Baker, Michael Milken, Alfred Taubman, Andrew Fastow, Bill Clinton, Martha Stewart and the Roman Catholic Church, Arthur Andersen, ENRON, TYCO, WORLDCOM, ADELPHI, even Bank of America. They shake our confidence, that's what. They shake our trust which is so essential to preserve our healthy society. Are we Americans too forgiving, too accepting?

We should remember that dishonesty is wrong, even if it is legal. Moral indignation is essential to fight selfish abuse of authority. Silence is tantamount to acquiescence.

As I get older, I realize more and more all one has, in a final evaluation, is one's integrity. To live a truthful life, I try to follow my "inner voice of good" before choosing a particular course of action.

If we do nothing to stop the escalating violation of ethical standards, whether in our trade or elsewhere, we will find:

- more cheating and violence in schools
- more tax evasion
- more lying ("For Wall Street, lying comes easily" headlined the *Washington Post* in 1991)
- a drop in the caliber of public officials
- more scandals, more sleaze.

I have been fortunate to be in the jewelry business, where our products are symbols of love, beauty, history and happiness. We have brought smiles and joy to millions of people who have trusted us. Let that trust not disappear.

Jimmy Carter once promised us, "for better or for worse, America will get a Government as good as its people."

Please, for better.

MY RIGHT HAND

The division of executive duties is very simple. I do what I want. Everything else is her responsibility. It is very fair and not at all onerous because my right hand, Nancy Spitzer, is a "can- do" woman.

Nancy is tall and blonde, personable and artistic with a confident and endearing manner.

In January of 1985, she applied to us for a part-time position. She had excellent credentials and had worked in the jewelry industry for twenty years. A previous employer recommended her by saying that even if we didn't need her then, we should employ her, before someone else did.

Ms Spitzer had a number of requests. She didn't want to work weekends, didn't want to work on the sales floor and wanted a few days a week to pursue her primitive folk art.

I wanted her to work on our busiest day, Saturday; her pleasant personality was such I could see her excelling in sales; I preferred her to work full time.

I employed her anyway.

It's now nearly twenty years since Nancy Spitzer and I have been colleagues. Every five years we celebrate. After ten years we commissioned a famous calligrapher who prepared an exquisite illuminated manuscript in her honor. She reminds me, in count-down fashion, of every upcoming anniversary.

It's like my wife's reminder before her birthday: "only eighteen days to go." One year I made a big mistake with Zelda. I told her to choose an appropriate piece of jewelry from the store. She let me have it. "It's your selection of a gift, your message on the card, your thought process and your effort that make my birthday special." That night I came home to a beautiful gift-wrapped box from Neiman Marcus with a card reading: "To Zelda, my bright, beautiful and beloved wife: Many happy returns! All my love." There was no signature, only a peel-off sticker which read "sign here" with an arrow instructing me where I should write my name. I never went that route again.

Nancy started her employment with us on a half-day basis with typing and filing duties. We were so busy we needed more of her time. She obliged and took over the job of telephone operator. Whatever she did, she did well and I was thrilled with her appointment.

Our business had millions of dollars in inventory, much of it in small valuables with a tendency to "have legs." Tight stock control was essential. I felt Nancy should be promoted to taking care of this procedure and organizing the biannual physical stock count, an event which took a week to finalize. In our early days, each item of inventory was photographed on to an "A" sheet where it was numbered and described in great detail. Every diamond, every piece of jewelry and silver was entered into the computer with information about when and where we bought it, the metal, the weight, the measurements, the stone information, costs price, selling price, etc. Reconciliation was difficult because we had stock out on consignment, stock at repair facilities, prepaid stock for overseas purchases, etc. Nancy was up to the challenge of controlling the stock monster, for such it was, eating up storage costs, insurance costs and interest costs each day.

When Nancy started at Heller Jewelers we had about twenty employees, mostly sales associates, but also a bookkeeper and an assistant bookkeeper, two goldsmiths, and a repair clerk, a gemologist-appraiser and a maid. Nancy exhibited leadership qualities and could converse with clients and staff with authority. We could trust her. She was promoted to Manager and given the keys and codes.

I saw so many appraisals of other jewelers that were poorly done, that I decided to check every one of ours myself. That was a real burden for me as we did hundreds and hundreds of appraisals each year and I read every word for accuracy.

At first we were not totally computerized and Nancy typed appraisals on an electric typewriter from the longhand of the gemologist. She typed and typed and typed. It is amazing to think back on those days without a word processor. As time went by, so did the workload and the appraisals were delegated to someone else.

I always believed in an open-door policy with my staff to handle any suggestions or difficulties. I had few secrets from my colleagues and management decisions were explained.

Nancy was involved more and more with these decisions like what we should buy, how we should market, who should we appoint. As an artist, she took particular pride in the window and showcase displays. She was a jack-of-all-trades and excelled in many segments of the business. She was very handy and did things like covering the back boards for the displays and attending to office machinery repairs. Nothing was too much trouble to get the job done.

Running an out of state jewelry show is very different from an in-store operation. Nancy was sent to shows in Dallas, Miami, New York and Las Vegas and performed admirably every time.

Our clients were very special to us. They bought beautiful pieces of jewelry or silver from us, so we tried to accommodate them in many ways. Nancy has been with ladies in their living rooms, dressing rooms, kitchens and fitting rooms of fine stores.

One person for whom we did a multi-million dollar appraisal, expressed a need to organize her large safe at home. "I can do that," Nancy said. She measured the safe and then crafted a shell to hold dozens of trays holding bracelets, brooches, rings, necklaces, etc. When she arrived at the home to install her creation and sort out the jewelry, she was let in and told she would be alone in the house and should lock the safe when finished and close the front door. She had millions of dollars of jewelry spread out on the upstairs landing from one end to the other. After labeling the trays and placing each piece of jewelry in its own compartment, she felt very pleased this project had worked out so beautifully. A couple of years later she returned to the same house, let herself in as instructed, photographed and took notes of all the silver pieces for an extensive appraisal.

On a number of occasions a client would want an item of jewelry custom-made using their stones. Nancy, the designer, would make a sketch and set their stones or our stones in a wax layout so that they could get a good idea of the final piece before any work was done. This little project made a big difference in how the clients made up their mind, and in most cases left no doubt how the piece would look. She enjoyed using our large selection of loose colored stones and diamonds to create items for our inventory.

In 1988 and again in 1989 I asked Nancy to do a primitive folk art painting to be used on a Thanksgiving card and sent to our clients. The two paintings she produced were just what I wanted. The first card was an autumn farm scene. The subsequent card has an old mill with a water wheel and the mill is titled "Victory Mills," the name of our grain business in South Africa. We had many favorable comments from our clients and she received several commissions. One lady wanted an active scene in an old farm kitchen. She actually gave Nancy a long list of all the things she wanted in the picture.

At Heller Jewelers each day brought something different, from actually holding a piece of Paul Revere silver to packing twelve trunks to be shipped to an out-of-state jewelry show, as we unpacked we found candies and other goodies she had tucked in the packing, or finding a quiet and private place for a mother to nurse her baby. These years were good ones and I have much admiration and respect for Nancy Spitzer who help make them special and often, fun.

Without being asked, Nancy has taken care of my thirst and hunger in the store. Not to mention my occasional need for chocolate. Iced or hot water, as the season prescribed, was always on hand, courtesy of Nancy. Everyday at noon she took my lunch order. Panera Caesar salad, Cosi mozzarella and tomato sandwich, Maggiano's chicken, or Chinese bean curd and veggies – it was my call. Before the hour was out, my meal appeared.

In my previous life in South Africa, I had a great secretary, Jean Holloway. She was with me for twenty-one years and there were tears all round when I emigrated. I felt sure I would never find another colleague who could be so helpful.

I was wrong. In America, I found the other woman in my life, a gem, my right hand, Nancy Spitzer.

NANCY SPITZER

THE 1988 THANKSGIVING CARD

THE 1989 THANKSGIVING CARD

NANCY SPITZER

YOU HAVE BEEN AN OUTSTANDING
EMPLOYEE FOR TEN YEARS
rendering devoted and trustworthy
service of a high order, commanding
the respect of your peers, being a
credit to the jewelry profession
with your knowledge, versatility and
performance; acting as a worthy
ambassador of our firm, displaying
an upbeat personality in the midst
of the pressures of business.

WE EXPRESS OUR HEARTFELT THANKS
AND SINCERE BEST WISHES &
WE SALUTE YOU AS
A PRECIOUS GEM

HELLER

Karl Heller   *Frada Heller*
KARL HELLER   FRADA HELLER

JANUARY, NINETEEN HUNDRED AND NINETY-FIVE

CERTIFICATE OF APPRECIATION

GO WELL!

In these pages of anecdotal confessions, I have tried to impart the flavor of an upscale jewelry establishment in the nation's capital. These tales of my life on the job comprise a memoir of my years as a jeweler.

The friendly atmosphere in our store made it conducive to being a meeting place for friends to enjoy a cup of tea. We all gossiped. Everyone's financials, political affiliations, love affairs, fashion statements, divorces and pregnancies were discussed. We were confidants, indeed even voyeurs posing as jewelers.

Over the years we have served generation after generation and have always valued the confidence placed with us. We have learned a lot from those who visited us. The relationship with our clients transcends the commercial. We felt that the bond of friendship became personal and often intellectual.

Now that my exciting but all-consuming career in retail jewelry is over, I have time to think and indeed tackle other projects, things that I enjoy, like writing, reading, working for charities and developing land. Zelda and I hope to travel more. There is a full schedule.

Psychiatrists tell us that FEAR, more than sex or food, is the prime motivational factor. We fear death, the loss of loved ones, jobs, health, money, status, public respect and many other things. I try to fight fear and subscribe to the phrase "cowards die a thousand times before their death, the valiant taste of death but once." So my response to fear is to go for anything worthy of experiencing.

I am happy with my lot. I enjoy the journey. Doing nothing is unthinkable. I do not intend to retire. I like challenges. My favorite word is "EUREKA"! I want to be involved and leave this planet a little better than when I was placed on it. If heaven exists, I would like God to welcome me with the words: "Good job, Old Man!"

Thank you for reading this.

Go well!

About the Author

Prior to settling in Washington, D.C. in 1980, Israel Heller was CEO of an agribusiness conglomerate in South Africa. In the U.S. he changed his career to that of jeweler. Twenty-one years later, he phased out of retailing. He lectures on diamonds and silver.

He co-authored *Deadly Truth*, a novel set in the Apartheid era.

He and his wife have two children and four grandchildren.

His interests include travel, golf, fly-fishing and land development.